The Power of One

It's Your Move

Jay Strack

Pat Williams

The Power of ONE - It's Your Move.

(The Success Secrets of Shamgar – 2nd Edition: Revised and Updated)

Copyright © 2024 by Jay Strack and Pat Williams

All rights reserved. No part of this book may be reproduced or transmitted in any form or by any means without written permission from the authors.

Unless otherwise noted, Scriptures are from New International Version, published by Biblica, 1978, 1984, 2011.

ISBN: 979-8-218-98629-2

Printed in the USA by Student Leadership University
Orlando, Florida
www.slulead.com

Cover photo courtesy of Allison Saeng
allisonsaeng@gmail.com
behance.net/allisonsaeng

PRAISE for The Power of One

"I have known Jay Strack for more than three decades. He has preached at Prestonwood Church more times than I can count, and we host his outstanding Youth Pastors Summits. Pat Williams was a godly, inspiring man of God. Their stories of overcoming the odds and the many that fill this book will motivate you to rise up and go for the call of God on your life with excellence."

Dr. Jack Graham, Sr. Pastor
Prestonwood Church

The Power of One will prove to be a classic. Although the principles are simple, the book is anything but simplistic. Applying these principles will prove to be a transforming experience in your life."

Dwight "Ike" Reighard
CEO, Must Ministries

"Jay Strack and Pat Williams are two of the most inspirational people I know. They have hit their highest level with this book on Shamgar. It's going to become an inspirational classic."

Coach Dave Wannstedt,
FOX Sports Football Studio Analyst

Jay Strack knows about risk, dreaming, and accomplishing goals and Pat Williams spent his life motivating others to do so. *The Power of One* shares how to overcome the pain of the past and encourages the reader to do the same no matter the circumstances.

Dr. Tim Clinton, President,
American Association of Christian Counselors

I dedicate THE POWER OF ONE
to my
Remarkable, Compassionate, Amusing, Grandchildren.
Lovers of Jesus and "Neighbors,"
You are Gifts to my Soul.
Gabriel, Charis, Mercy, Za'Riah, Zi'Yon, Ariana.

As this book went to press,
my dear friend and brother, **PAT WILLIAMS**,
suddenly departed for eternity.
He will be sorely missed by the thousands upon
thousands he has inspired, encouraged, and loved.
I am one of them.
His influence will live on for generations to come, and
his writings will bolster your dreams

Jay Strack

TABLE of CONTENTS

INTRODUCTION: Firt Things First 9
ONE: Start Where You Are – Jay Strack 11
    God Shows Up 18
    Definition of Success 22
    Never Despise Small Beginnings 34
TWO: Use What You Have – Pat Williams 41
    Is War Ever Justified? 41
    The Sacred NOW 46
THREE: The Power of One – Jay Strack 55
    Opportunity: Grab it or Lose it 65
    The Reality of the Enemy 68
    Legacy Lives and Breathes 70
    Think Cumulatively 76
FOUR: Your Ox Goad – Pat Williams 83
    Seven Resources You Already Have 87
FIVE: The Practice of Creativity – Jay Strack 119
    Think Creatively! 124
    Be Inspired Every Day 141
    Creativity is Our Birthright 145

SIX: Your Life Mission – Pat Williams	151
Pray	155
Think	163
Set Goals	167
Work Hard	173
Compete Intensely	178
Persevere	181
Serve Others	187
SEVEN: Cancel the Noise – Jay Strack	193
You Are Chosen	198
Low-Intensity Winning	203
Listen for the Call of God	206
Keep Cotton in Your Pocket	210
The Gift of Sacrifice	217
No Excuses	223
EPILOGUE: It's Your Move	229
About the Authors	235
Endnotes	237

INTRODUCTION

First Things First

One of the great themes of the Bible is:
"God can do anything, you know—far more than you could ever imagine, guess, or request in your wildest dreams! He does it not by pushing us around but by working within us, His Spirit deeply and gently within us." Ephesians 3:20 - The Message

As you turn each page, you will sense a common invitation of the prophets, Jesus, and the early disciples as the ministry grew - "Come and see…" what God can do. He will "work within" you as you dare to imagine and trust in the plethora of His promises. **Success by definition is determined by your willingness to discover the purpose the Creator has planned for your life.**

Begin with self-assessment: "Where am I right now? Am I stuck, behind, is something's missing? Is there a habit that needs to be started or one that needs to be broken?" Being honest with yourself is the beginning of life's adventures and understanding God's will.

Join Pat Williams and Jay Strack on a journey to the future by way of the life-altering stories of history's courageous heroes and heroines.

ONE

Start Where You Are

- Jay Strack

"When something is important enough, you do it even if the odds are not in your favor."
Elon Musk

The story of a hero named Shamgar, tucked away in the Old Testament Book of Judges, is often overlooked. Though we don't know much about him, we can make some valid assumptions about his character. His biography reads he *"struck down 600 Philistines with an ox goad. He too saved Israel."* (Judges 3:31). As impressive as this feat is, we do not understand how Shamgar pulled off such a grand win.

The story of the great Hebrew lawgiver and liberator, Moses, fills 136 chapters of the Bible. The story of Joseph, a model of absolute integrity, occupies 21 chapters of the Bible. The life of Jesus—the most significant leader, teacher, and prophet in history—is recorded in the first 89 chapters of the New Testament. Indeed, it is essential to understand these leaders' stories, backgrounds, and characters. But Shamgar, who is attributed to saving Israel, is given only two verses. Shamgar could have used a better marketing agent.

You're probably wondering, "How important could Shamgar be if that's all the mention he gets? What can I learn from a guy whose entire biography consists of forty-two words?" Read on, my friend, and you'll be amazed at what Shamgar can teach you about successful, influential living.

The Holy Spirit deliberately chose every word in the Scriptures to impact our lives with wisdom, encouragement, and understanding. Through those two little verses, God tells us that there is no limit to what we can achieve if we learn and apply the simple lessons of Shamgar's legacy.

After Ehud came Shamgar son of Anath, who struck down 600 Philistines with an ox goad. He too saved Israel. (Judges 3:31)

"In the days of Shamgar son of Anath, in the days of Jael, the highways were abandoned; travelers took to winding paths. (Judges 5:6)

According to several Bible dictionaries, the name Shamgar means "stranger."[1] Perhaps this speaks to his heritage as a "son of Anath," the goddess of war and helpmate to Baal.[2] At first blush, it seems complicated to understand how the Canaanite goddess Anath and a judge of Israel could be mentioned in the same sentence. Judges 3 tells us that the Israelites lived among the Canaanites, Hittites, Amorites, Perizzites, Hivites, and

Jebusites. They took their daughters in marriage, gave daughters to the Canaanite sons, and served their gods.[2] Shamgar was possibly born of both an Israelite and a Canaanite parent. From one of them, he may have heard of Joshua's proclamation to the Israelites: *"But if serving the Lord seems undesirable to you, then choose for yourselves this day whom you will serve, whether the gods your ancestors served beyond the Euphrates, or the gods of the Amorites, in whose land you are living. But as for me and my household, we will serve the Lord."* (Joshua 24:15). At some point, Shamgar learned of the One True God of Israel and chose to follow and serve Him.

What we don't know isn't important because it is a fact that God used Shamgar to save Israel. The background through the book of Judges reminds us that the Lord can and does use anyone. Throughout ancient history, the Scriptures reveal narratives of unlikely heroes and heroines. Your "pedigree," where you are from, who your family is, the past you inherited or chose – none of it matters to Him. Step up and follow through when the Faithful God calls you to serve.

At the beginning of my Christian life, I knew nothing of the Bible other than my life was radically changed by the phrase, "Jesus, I believe. Here is my life." Spiritual and emotional bondage brings enemies into every part of life. I had no job, future, family support, or idea of what was next. When I learned the miracle of Shamgar's victory and the truth of such a great God, a fire exploded in me. I pray that the Holy Spirit will fill you with that same fire of courageous confidence to face the future as you read, reflect, pray, and think about the man named Shamgar who prevailed against impossible odds.

The Philistines' strategy was to invade and destroy the fields that sustained the Israelite villagers by setting fires in the night. As word spread among the tents, the Israelite men dashed out to protect their crops. Meanwhile, the enemy would take the women and children hostage to torture and murder them while the men were out. It could have been a night just like that caused Shamgar to say, "Enough is enough. I will go out and slay them on my own."

Like Shamgar, there will come a moment when you realize it is your turn to rise and make a difference in a life, a community, a church, a company, the culture, or the nation. Will you be ready?

Judges 2:10 tells us that the great Hebrew forefathers were long dead when Shamgar was born. *"After that whole generation had been gathered to their ancestors, another generation grew up who knew neither the Lord nor what he had done for Israel."* The Israelites found themselves in need of a king or valid leadership. It was a time of oppression and depression as people trudged through a daily life of poverty without a promise of opportunity. All of us have, at times, felt depressed

THE POWER OF ONE

by a lack of opportunity, indecisive leadership, or a daily grind that seems to go nowhere. That is normal as long as it is temporary. In those moments, you must rise and take ownership of the promises of the Faithful God who is capable and willing to do more than you can imagine.

After the death of Joshua, Israel's great military leader, the land of Israel was overrun by terrorists. Judges 5:6 describes the days of Shamgar as evil and dangerous times. *"In the days of Shamgar, son of Anath, in the days of Jael, the highways were abandoned; travelers took to winding paths."* The people avoided the known roads for fear of the bandits, such as the Philistines, who were the Al Qaeda, ISIS, Hamas, Hezbollah, and Houthis of their day. With no central government or standing army, Israel was vulnerable on every side. Those were lawless times, and the Hebrew people were leaderless and defenseless.

Shamgar was most likely a farmer who used his ox goad to strike down the "600 Philistines." An ox goad is a cattle prod, a long wooden pole tipped with a sharpened iron point at one end and capped with a flattened chisel-like iron blade at the other. Farmers used the ox goad's sharp point to poke the tough hide when livestock slowed their plow pulling. The blade end was used to scrape the roots, thorns, and accumulated clay. Compare this type of quiet life to that of the barbarous, violent Philistines.

We know that Shamgar lived in Canaan more than 3,000 years ago. The land comprised dozens of walled-city states, and multiple cultures lived there, constantly at war. The Hebrews migrated to the Promised Land after generations of bondage under the pharaohs of Egypt, as promised by God in Genesis chapter 15 and Joshua chapter 1.

After the death of Moses, the servant of the Lord, the Lord said to Joshua, son of Nun, Moses' aide: *"Moses my servant is dead. Now then, you and all these people, get ready to cross the Jordan River into the land I am about to give to them—to the Israelites. I will give you every place where you set your foot, as I promised Moses.* (Joshua1:2-3)

Philistia consisted of an alliance of five Philistine cities—Ashkelon, Ashdod, Gath, Gaza, and Ekron. The antagonism between Ancient Israel and the Philistines continued for centuries until King David and beyond. Wars between these factions have continued throughout millennia. As you know from the current news, the more things change, the more they remain the same for Israel and Palestine.

Many believe that when the Romans subjugated the land of Israel, they named it "Palaestínia" (the Latin form of the word "Philistia") deliberately insulting the Jewish people by calling their homeland after their worst enemies.[3] Today, the Palestinian Arabs claim to be descendants of the Philistines. However, the Philistines originally came to the Gaza region from the Aegean Islands and settled on the southern coast of Palestine in

THE POWER OF ONE

the 12th century, about the time of the arrival of the Israelites.[4] Hence, this claim has no historical basis.

Before Shamgar defeated the Philistines and saved Israel, no one would have picked him as a man destined for greatness. He was a clod-kicker with dirt under his fingernails and ox manure on the soles of his sandals. No one would have looked at him and said, "There's the man who's going to save our nation." Yet this little-known farmer single-handedly did just that, wiping out 600 Philistine warriors and saving the nation. Shamgar demonstrated more military savvy than Gen. George S. Patton, Gen. Stormin' Norman Schwarzkopf, U.S. Seal Team Leaders, and Special Forces Commanders combined!

The story and messages of Shamgar began impacting me early in my Christian life and continue to inspire me decades later. Over and over, the Lord sent me new, healthy relationships who spoke to me of the life of Shamgar. These truths and those who taught them have remained with me for a lifetime as a powerful, continual motivation. "Keep going, Jay," I would tell myself on the most challenging days. "If Shamgar can do it, you can do it."

Together, let us walk through history and personal experiences to win life's battles with courageous faith. You will see yourself in various pages of this book – perhaps not in exact circumstances, but through similar emotions of nervous fear, apprehension over the future, and relationships that may falter. We will journey from impossible to *"God can do anything you know."*

Throughout this book, you will find many stories of modern and historical Shamgars who had little to start with, odds against them, and obstacles blocking the finish line. If you imagine your own life in each story and note how one person can impact the life of another, you will be inspired and encouraged to live with consistent integrity and strong hope for the future. Life is a system of giving and receiving. We receive encouragement and then encourage others; we receive inspiration and then inspire; we receive wisdom from Scripture and share wisdom from Scripture; and as you sacrifice for others, others will sacrifice for you. These accumulate one at a time into a life of fulfillment and purpose, of favor with man and God. Solomon reminds us:

Let love and faithfulness never leave you; bind them around your neck, write them on the tablet of your heart. Then you will win favor and a good name in the sight of God and man. (Proverbs 3:3-4)

God Shows Up

The best definition of "coincidence" I have heard was from my friend who sticks closer than a brother, Dr. Ike Reighard. He said, "A coincidence is when God chooses to remain anonymous." As I thought that definition through, it hit me that many "coincidences" have saved my life. I still can't get over the incredible choice of a nerdy kid named Charlie to talk about a "real" Jesus and pray daily for the junkie who ignored him most of the time. And what are the odds that I would randomly be released from the juvenile detention center, hitchhike to the beach, and in those aimless moments a guy I never met would swim up to deliver a personal message from Jesus to me? Were those random flukes or was each move orchestrated by the God who loved me? Having lived many days in the Land of Coincidence since then, I am confident God showed up for me.

What are the odds that I would make it to adulthood let alone graduate from Charleston Southern University Cum Laude. How did a former junkie earn a doctorate; receive three honorary doctorates; speak in schools across America; conduct area-wide crusades; speak to pro sports teams, and found Student Leadership University, the ministry that trains students to become influential leaders? How did an ADD, dyslexic drug addict who couldn't get out of his own way have the privilege of sharing a message of hope, success, and fulfillment with audiences across the country and around the world? At best, those were 600-to-one odds. Shamgar odds.

I share my story only to boast of the God Who loves "second chancers" like me. The opportunities that have come to me were delivered through the free-flowing grace of God, available to anyone who asks for it. There is no chance that without Him I would have won any of life's battles, reached my goals, or influenced lives.

We all face overwhelming odds in one way or another, not just when we pursue our grand dreams, but often when we are simply trying to survive the battles of daily life. Perhaps the most crucial relationship in your life is falling apart; you are facing unbearable losses; someone you love is in pain; finances are tight; or you are on the edge of emotional bankruptcy. You know what you are up against. Whatever you are facing today, you don't have to be defeated. You can overcome 600-to-one odds. If Shamgar could do it, if Jay Strack could do it, you can do it. You can overcome life's odds because Jesus already has.

My daughter, Missy, has bravely battled through physical disabilities. Scoliosis required a brace for years and later surgery; hearing impairment is helped some by wearing hearing aids daily; and surgery for eye muscle issues forced her into glasses even as a baby. One day, when she was about 8, I heard her crying in the stairwell and a thump-thump-thump alongside. Jumping to her aid, I found her body-slamming the brace, holding the glasses and the hearing aids in her hand, ready to throw them down. "I am tired of this stuff, Daddy. I feel like an experiment. Please don't make me wear these anymore." I wept with her and asked the Lord for wisdom. I knew this "stuff" was essential and not optional. "Missy, Daddy loves you just the way you are.

THE POWER OF ONE

You are a gift from God to me." She took a breath and asked, "Really Daddy? Then I can throw them away?" Holding back tears, I replied, "No honey. I love you just the way you are, but I love you too much to leave you that way."

The reason that answer came to me so quickly was that I felt the Savior had said the same to me. All my "stuff" did not stop His love, but change was imperative for me to find a successful, confident future. The same goes for you: He loves you too much to leave you the way you are.

P.S. –Missy has become a lovely, courageous, godly woman. As a teen, she adopted James 1:2-3 as her life verses: *"Consider it pure joy, my brothers and sisters, whenever you face trials of many kinds, because you know that the testing of your faith produces perseverance."* Missy is inspiring to all she meets.

The first step in finding success in life is to hammer out a working definition of success. Start by doing an assessment Q & A with yourself.

- What are you aiming for?
- What does it look like for you to overcome in life?
- How much are you willing to sacrifice time, energy, or popularity?
- Why do you give up or give in?

After you have carefully thought the answers through and answered honestly, write them down. This is an essential step because as you study and pray over these, the Lord will clarify them. Knowing what you are aiming for is essential to winning the battle. Before I share any more of my life's "600-to-one odds" (and believe me, there are many), allow me to share three personal definitions of success that others have modeled for me. I hope you will find at least one worthy of living by and passing on to others.

Definition of Success

My first definition of success was gifted to me as a 21-year-old student at Charleston Southern University. The school President, Dr. John A. Hamrick, assigned me to host and drive the G.O.A.T. motivational speaker, Zig Ziglar, to various speaking engagements around the school and the Charleston area. I was ecstatic and probably talked way too much out of nervousness. After a few days of me trying to be cool, Zig turned to look me in the eye, placed his hand on my shoulder, and said in his unique Southern drawl, "Jay, if you want your dreams to come true, then you must be willing to help others make their dreams come true."

The friendship that was birthed that day was a great gift and privilege. For decades I watched Zig live that definition. The example of Zig Ziglar worked its way into the call on my life. Because of his advice, I began telling my story of overcoming broken homes, drug addiction and ADD learning challenges in high schools across America. Those led to churches and then area and city-wide crusades. And then I was called to teach biblical worldview and servant leadership to students. Almost 30 years and some 300,000 attendees later, listening to dreamers and thinking through steps to goals together continues to be one of the great joys of my life.

Almost every week, people call me to share, "I was a success in reaching my goals and went even beyond what I imagined." Recently, a young man texted to say that while attending SLU at 17, he wrote that his dream was to be a songwriter. His song recently hit the top 10 in country music. There were a lot of naysayers along the way, but this guy wasn't willing to give up. Against the odds, he won.

The second definition of success came to me more than a decade after college when I was privileged to preach at the church John Maxwell pastored in San Diego. You may know John as a New York Times bestselling author who has sold millions upon millions of his 40+ books, but I know him as a guy with a heart for sharing the Gospel. Over the years, I listened to every one of his recorded messages I could find and bought every book as it came out. Along the way, John has become a dear friend and brother. I can say from personal experience that there is not a selfish bone in John Maxwell – he is about generosity, training, listening, caring, and serving men and women across the globe. He is one of my spiritual heroes. John stepped in to promote Student Leadership University when we first began without being asked, without ever asking for a thing in return.

I recently spent a day in the studio with John, the undisputed G.O.A.T. of leadership training, as he mentored global leaders online. It was a remarkable experience to behold. John's friendship is a great privilege for me, and his definition of success has become a lifelong goal. He said, "Jay, success is when those who know you the best love you the most." John went on to explain, "It's not about how much money you make, a prestigious career, a fancy car, or a big house. Do your friends and family love you the most.?" That is a completely different paradigm from the six broken homes I grew up in. John's few words may sound like easy success at first, but at a time when 50% of marriages are crumbling and frivolous lawsuits over who did what to whom fill courts, crushing ends to relationships say otherwise. Authentic success isn't about making a good public impression. To be truly successful, you must be a person of genuine integrity, character, and positive influence in the home, workplace, and community, day in and day out. By that standard, the people who know you best—your family and close friends—are qualified to define your success. Healthy friendships are an integral part of dreams coming to fruition.

A very long shelf in my library is crammed full and overflowing with John's books, but his *"21 Irrefutable*

THE POWER OF ONE

Laws of Leadership," sits prominently on the corner of my desk. Even though page after page is earmarked and circled with "aha" thoughts, it is John's simple definition of success that I carry with me daily.

Both John and Zig, and a host of others along life's way, have shown me that "hand-me-down" hope is a lifeline for all of us to receive and to give. And often, it makes the difference in a marriage, a career, a goal, or emotional/spiritual health.

As doors of opportunity continued to open, I had to ask myself, "What is the key to continuing to beat the odds? And how do I know I am in the right lane going forward?" These questions led me to my third and personal definition of success. In every choice, decision, challenge, or rejoicing, Matthew 6:33 must reign:

"But seek first his kingdom and his righteousness, and all these things will be given to you as well." For me, the verse translates to the rule: *"Say 'yes' to God's best."*

Step by step, a dream takes shape. Sometimes it ends up more successful than you imagined; other times, it morphs into a different goal. Many of our SLU alums work in politics, are generous givers through successful businesses, have healthy families and relationships, lead in the military, grow effective ministries and churches, or are foreign missionaries in lands of danger as they serve people and share the Gospel. As adults, they are living out the goals they said "yes" to as students.

I started from behind with fewer resources than Shamgar had. When you read my challenges and mistakes, you may see yourself or someone you know. Jay Strack's pain and blunders serve as testimonies of God's elegant grace and mercy that support everyone who chooses to start over again. I am confident that if I can overcome a bad start, anyone can.

A successful businessman, my father was listed in Who's Who, but he was so seldom home that we all said, "Who's he?" He was chairman of the board everywhere but in our home. Publicly my father was seen as a success; at home, we knew a different person, a raging alcoholic. At least once a week, Dad thundered in anger for an hour or so and then threatened to leave us. Mom cowered and cried in the corner, and I hid under my bed, covering my ears and holding my breath until it was over. When I was six years old, the fighting came to an end. "There is no reason for me to stay," Dad barked after a heated argument. Hugging the 6'2' former soldier around the knees I cried, "If you need a reason, Dad, let me be your reason to stay, please!" Without a response, as if I hadn't said a word, my father walked out the door, dragging my little body as he went. When he jumped into the car I saw another woman in the front seat, but still I chased after him. When he came to a red light, I managed to catch up and bang on his window.

"Jay, go on. I mean it," he said in anger. He waved me off like a stray dog and sped away. I don't know how long I stood there, but I watched as he grew smaller and smaller and disappeared from my life.

Night after night, I prayed that God would send my father home, but it didn't happen. The message I got from my dad's abandonment was: "Jay, you're a loser. You're a nobody. You're not important to me or anyone else. I don't want you in my life." My mom dated many guys in the following years and went through several "marriages." Whether they were legal or staged for my benefit, I don't know, but over and over, Mom promised me a "real Dad." It was like living with a revolving door as Mom kept looking for the wrong guys in the wrong places. An alcoholic husband had already abandoned her, yet she kept going back to guys who were just like him or, worse, men she met in bars.

Note to single moms: You are not a "second-class" family. God has significant plans for you and your family. When you feel tempted to settle for mediocre, think of your children. They should not suffer from your decisions. Yes, aloneness is tough, but the big picture is that you can break the cycle of pain with your example of choosing healthy relationships. *"Those who hope in the Lord will renew their strength."* (Isa 40:31)

With each new guy Mom brought into the house, I dared to hope for a real family. Inevitably, each "stepdad" turned out to be a drunkard and abuser. On more than one occasion, I got out my Louisville Slugger baseball bat to warn some guy to quit hitting my mother—or to quit hitting me. Decades later, I still keep a ball bat in the corner of the nearby closet. Some instincts of the defense mode never stop. You may know what I am talking about.

The morning after a new "stepdad's" drunken tirades, I'd go to school and learn that talk of the loud brawl was already circulating. I tried to laugh it off, but inside I was dying of humiliation and hurt. After a while, men moving in and out of our house became almost normal; that is, until the summer when one of them brought his older son. That was the summer I learned about sexual abuse.

I wrote dozens of letters to my real dad, begging him to come and rescue me. He never came. He never answered my letters. Years later, as an adult, we talked about his alcoholic days, and I asked why he never responded to my letters. Dad said he never received any of them. "Likely story," I spitted out. A few years later, when Mom passed away, I learned the truth. Out of guilt and embarrassment, she never mailed them.

After six or so men moved in and out, one guy came who promised to stay. He married my mom and showed me the certificate. "Jay," he said, "you can call me Dad, and I will treat you like my own son." I was so excited to have a dad again that I went to school the next day and told all my friends about him. I bragged him up, telling my friends he played third base for the Yankees! But it wasn't long before Bob was out late drinking, just like all the rest.

Mom turned to me one night and said, "Jay, I am going to get Bob out of the bar. If he doesn't leave, I'm divorcing him!" I jumped into the car, believing I could keep her safe. We got to the bar, and she went inside while I waited. She came back quickly – alone and crying. I was eight years old, and I really wanted a dad. I was sure Bob would keep his word if I went in and reminded him, so I jumped out of the car, yelling "Mom, let me talk to him!" Before she could answer, I was standing in the doorway of the bar. The overwhelming smell of sweaty men, beer, and heavy smoke hit me right in the face, but I was not to be deterred from the mission. I was sure I could talk Bob into coming home, so I approached him at the bar counter where he was drinking with his shrimping buddies. "Jay, what the ………….. are you doing here?" With tears, I pleaded, "You promised to be my dad. Please come home. Mom is going to divorce you if you don't."

Bob laughed out loud as he told me, "If you get on your knees and beg me, I will come home." I fell to my knees, my hands in a prayer pose, and begged, "Please come home." Even as I spoke the words, Bob and everyone in the bar began laughing aloud as though they were watching a hilarious comedy. The light went out of my childhood that night, and I promised myself to never ask anyone for anything again.

Reading these childhood nightmares might bring up your own emotions of betrayal, hurt, misunderstanding, or abuse. If these thoughts come back to you, you have two choices:

1. Allow anger, fear, or hurt to be the lead dog of your emotions.
2. Work toward a positive future of healing as you shake off the dust of the past.

As the Knight told Indiana Jones, "Choose wisely, for while the true Grail will bring life, the false grail will take it from you.'

The Apostle Paul, suffering persecution and ridicule on every side wrote, *"Finally brothers and sisters, whatever is true, whatever is noble, whatever is right, whatever is pure, whatever is lovely, whatever is admirable—if anything is excellent or praiseworthy—think about such things."* (Philippians 4:8) That kind of thinking is a game changer.

It took a decade before I chose wisely. In the meantime, anger led my actions and reactions. I blamed God for the pain in my life, for the fact that my dad left us, for the alcoholic stepdads who battered me, for the violence in our home, for the "other woman" that ripped Dad from me, and for anything that left deep emotional scars. By the time I became a teenager, I had stopped blaming God because I stopped believing in God.

At school, comedy and laughter were my cover, but afterward the aloneness led me to keep seeking outrageous behavior. I craved the acceptance of the party crowd at school and in the neighborhood. The need to be accepted joined my loneliness to create a chain of bad choices. At 12, the gang offered me alcohol, and I gave up quickly on my promise not to do as Dad did. That led to smoking dope, popping pills, and then to the addiction of shooting speed. When I was high, I felt important and accepted. When I wasn't high, I felt like a nothing, a nobody.

Juvenile detention center lockups became my temporary home in and out over the summers. I dealt with it by staying high and covering my feelings with "Who cares?" but inside I was an empty kid without hope wishing that someone did care. My senior year was "iffy" as to whether I would graduate and skipping school became my norm. Out of nowhere, a guy named Charlie decided to share his newfound Jesus joy with me, and he did so every day that he saw me. He would wait for me by the locker, by the school entrance, near the gym, and anywhere he thought I might be. Charlie grew up in the church, but it was in the Jesus movement that his life was changed. At least that's what he told me. He started carrying his Bible to school and seemed happy all the time. I thought he was just crazy. No one could be happy all the time—not in this life.

I had Charlie in four classes during my senior year. I couldn't get away from the guy! At every turn, he would tell me, "Jay, you need Jesus!" He gave me booklets to read, but I couldn't understand and didn't want to. I was 17 years old and had never heard that God loved me or that Jesus died on the cross for my sins. Charlie approached me one day while my friends were with me, and that embarrassed me. I yelled at him, "Man, get away from me with all this Jesus stuff!" Charlie was hurt. He said, "If these guys were really your friends, they wouldn't want you to waste your life with drugs. They don't care what happens to you, but I do, and Jesus does." I couldn't grasp that idea, but it stuck in my mind. Could God really care about me? Why would he? My life was a mess—even my father didn't care about me.

On my sixth visit to the detention center, I was greeted with "Not you again!" Within an hour, I was placed into solitary so I couldn't get into fights. The room was silent, except for one loud voice. Over and over, I heard Charlie chant in my mind: "Jesus loves you." I hit the wall and looked out at the tiny square window. No hope. No escape. The words poured out of me in an angry challenge: "God, do you even know my name? Do you care about me? And if you are such a big deal, why don't you show yourself to me?" There were still no tears. Only darkness for the rest of the night.

For some reason, I was released early. Probably to get rid of me, but I asked no questions. My first thought was to hitchhike to the beach. On a borrowed surfboard,

I headed out to let the waves wash over me, but I was itching for a high. I had been out about 30 minutes when a guy paddled right up to me. This is against surfer protocol – you never go into another guy's space while surfing. I was glaring at him when he called out my name, "Jay!" I didn't remember seeing him around school or the neighborhood, but I was curious to know how he knew my name. "I know you don't know me. I just know of your rep at school. Hear me out – I know this sounds crazy, it does to me too, but I was leaving to go home, and Jesus said, "You remember the guy from your school? The one you just saw on the surfboard. Turn around, find him, and say that Jesus sent this message – 'He loves you. He knows your name. He has a plan for your life.'" I was speechless and in shock at that point. As he paddled away, tears flowed for the first time since I begged Bob in the bar to come home at the age of 8.

The uneasiness in me would not go away and after a few days, I gave in and made my way to the Bible study I had once rejected. I sat in the back, head down, hiding under my long hair. I had faced a lot of odds in my life, but this one was super personal. Somehow, I toned down my ADD enough to listen to the greatest story ever told. When the group leader read "*If God is for you, who can be against you?*" (Romans 8:31), it got my attention. He spoke of people in the Bible who did not start well but finished strong. "Could you be one of those?" he asked.

The flashback of kneeling in that bar and being laughed at kept haunting me. "How do I know God won't laugh? And that everyone in the room won't laugh?" It's hard to believe that a simple prayer from the heart can transform your life, but it did. Head still down, I heard the call to: "Stand if you want to give your life to Jesus." I shook inside and out for several minutes before a bolt of courage passed through me. I gave up on my past and stood in a moment of surrender to say, "Jesus, here is my messed-up life. Take it if you want."

God heard me, and I was changed. I would have never believed it myself had I not been there.

That night the sewers were flushed with drugs and alcohol as I emptied out my stash. The rats must have danced for a month! Think about it: No one told me, "Get rid of the drugs…". That is, no one with a voice you could hear. Was this a hallucination or reality? This tangible big first step told me it was all real.

Before we move on, I must ask—have you yielded to the God who cares deeply for you? It's simple, powerful, and life changing. With a few words of surrender, Jesus will swallow the pain of your past with the hope of your future.

Never Despise Small Beginnings

Early on in my ministry, I learned never to despise small beginnings. As an 18-year-old, I fell to my knees and cried before the Lord, "I will go anywhere you want me to go. I will do anything you want me to do." The following day, I got a call asking, "Jay, will you go and share your story?" I replied, "Yes!" before he said where and when.

"Great! I want you to go to Friendship Baptist Church in Immokalee, FL to about 15 people and preach." I was stunned at the quick answer to my prayer but didn't comprehend the word preach. And Immokalee? "Cowboys" and "hippies" did not mesh well in those days. Receiving an answer to my prayer bolstered me with courage. My fiancé, Diane, and I made our way to the little town, me with shoulder length hair and her in a long, floral hippie dress. Stopping into the mini mart for a Coke, I was confronted at the checkout with a challenge from the cowboy behind me. "Boy," he said, "you need a haircut."

Remember, I had not been a Christian long. Anger still sat right on the edge of my reactions. I didn't think twice about my answer as I glared back at him and said, "Why don't you grab some scissors, and we step outside. You up to it?" Diane whispered, "Jay, you are going to preach at a church just around the corner...." The cowboy and I stared at each other for a few minutes, and I walked out to the car, asking the Lord to forgive me as I drove away to the little church.

I share this story to remind you that spiritual maturity is like physical maturity. We all make mistakes as we grow. If we make it an essential part of our success story, we learn to respond rather than react. I am still learning.

Diane and I sat in the back pew, unrecognized and without welcome, for about 20 minutes. No one spoke to or glanced at the hippie couple who dared to enter the little white church. A man stood up and said, "Well, I guess Brother Fred forgot to send our preacher for today." I raised my hand and said, "It's me." Suddenly, there was a scramble as several huddled together in the corner to decide what to do. Then I heard them whisper, "Well, we only have a few minutes left anyway – how bad can it be?"

It never dawned on me to be upset that they did not accept me. This opportunity to tell the Good News was the driving force in my mind. Consider what drives you to react and what urges you to respond to the goal or person before you.

I stood up and told every verse I knew, which was not many, and threw in some I wasn't sure of. "Novice" and "inexperienced" were applicable as I waited for that ridiculing laughter that followed me since childhood. But afterward, people came to the altar with tears and began to pray. I was shocked and asked the music director, "How did you do that?" "Son," he replied. "You did that." I didn't know much about the Bible, but I knew immediately that I didn't "do" anything but present the Scripture and pray. Believe it or not, I was not only invited back, but they asked me to pastor the church. And, yes, I did cut my hair, but not because of the cowboy's threat. It was because I was beginning to understand what was important in life. When you have a heart to make a difference in the lives of others, to share the grace you have experienced, you decide to remove anything that will get in the way.

My new wife, Diane, and I spent the next year knocking on row after row of doors in the migrant camps and trailer parks as we prayed and shared about this Jesus we had just come to know. No one called us "successful" when doors were slammed shut in our faces; we lived in the small church trailer; preached to the tiny congregation; printed our handmade bulletins; mowed the lawn; and cleaned the church bathrooms and floors. My salary was less than $75 a week. But we felt successful. We knew we were a success when the Lord brought 106 people to salvation and baptism that first year.

Using the talent and resources God has given you and carrying out the unique mission God has assigned to you is another definition of success. We don't measure by hopeful results but by what we learn in the journey. When you seek God's will for your life, you will always succeed in God's eyes, even if the culture and the world's ideas define you as a failure.

Because I was willing to "go anywhere you want me to go," the Lord took me from a small, remote congregation to experiencing the privilege of traveling to

28 countries, sharing a message of hope with 10,000 public high schools and with the leaders of such organizations as Walmart, Johnson & Johnson, Chick-fil-A, the U.S. Air Force Academy, and NASA; to NBA and NFL teams. Decade after decade, the message has not changed.

Know this: Starting where you are does not determine the outcome of your goal. It is the first step in the adventure as you Use What You Have. When you act on these Biblical success principles, you will find that God takes you way beyond what you first asked for and above what you imagined. Start now to believe that every day, every choice matters. If you give up and surrender to the battle in front of you, you end up wherever the enemy decides to put you.

Now, may I introduce you to Pat Williams, a dear friend, who left suddenly for eternity as this book was being published in a 2nd Edition. I have known Pat for decades and watched his integrity in high-def, 4K color. There is not one particular phrase I could share from Pat because there are hundreds in my study notes, and many are repeated throughout this book. When we got together for dinner, the stories and thoughts flowed, and I took notes all the way through. He was one of the most positive, humble, tenacious, faithful, godly, focused men I have known. Pat's stories will amaze you and then set you afire with inspiration. He has shown me and thousands more how to overcome the ODDS.

THE POWER OF ONE

Beyond what I have known about my dear friend, allow me to share what the NBA has written about Pat Williams: "He built the 1983 championship team in Philadelphia and brought pro basketball to central Florida with the Orlando Magic. He raised a family of 19 children, 14 of whom were adopted from overseas. He has run more than 50 marathons and is a mountain climber who has scaled Mt. Rainier. Pat Williams was the recipient of the John Bunn Lifetime Achievement award." My friend, Pat Williams, was the ultimate Shamgar of this generation, and he will be greatly missed.

TWO

Use What you Have

- Pat Williams

"When you have exhausted all possibilities, remember this - you haven't." Thomas Edison

I knew that prayer had given me the courage to hope beyond hope.

Looking back, there is no question in my mind that the Orlando Magic exists in large part because my colleagues and I were operating by the three success secrets of Shamgar. Perhaps building an NBA franchise is not as big an accomplishment as, say, wiping out 600 Philistines with an ox goad and saving an entire nation, but I think we did all right. And our accomplishment illustrates what ordinary people can do when they follow the pattern that was laid down by this man from ancient Israel.

Is War Ever Justified?

The spirit of Shamgar permeates throughout history. Alvin C. York was the Shamgar of World War

I. His incredible story is told in the National Museum of the. United States Army. Born in a log cabin in the tiny village of Pall Mall, Tennessee, in 1887, Alvin helped his father on the farm and spent a lot of time hunting in the woods. As a teenager, Alvin gained a reputation as a deadly marksman. He could plug the eye of a turkey at a hundred yards.

But as Alvin York moved through his late teens and into his twenties, he developed a reputation as a hell-raiser. The townspeople of Pall Mall agreed that Alvin would never amount to anything. He had a definite taste for whiskey, gambling, and brawling in bars.

All of that changed suddenly in 1914 when Alvin's best friend, Everett Delk, was killed in a bar fight just over the state line, in Static, Kentucky. Suddenly, Alvin was brought face to face with the brevity of life and the reality of death. Soon afterward, he astonished his neighbors when he walked into a revival meeting where the Rev. H. H. Russell of the Church of Christ in Christian Union was preaching. When Brother Russell invited people to come forward and give their lives to Christ, Alvin walked forward.

Immediately, Alvin York was a changed man. He was baptized and joined the church, becoming a Sunday school teacher and the church choir leader.

Alvin's commitment to the church's strict rules of "no war" was severely tested when the United States declared war on Germany in 1917. Alvin received a draft

THE POWER OF ONE

notice, which he returned to the draft board with these words scrawled across the back: "Don't want to fight." He was denied conscientious objectors because his church was not a recognized pacifist sect, like the Quakers or Mennonites. He reported to Camp Gordon, Georgia, and went through basic training, where he astonished his superiors with his ability as a marksman. Still, he stubbornly insisted that he would never aim his rifle at another human being.

After a series of long talks with his battalion commander, Alvin York was persuaded that war, though horrible and tragic, was sometimes a moral necessity to free innocent people from tyranny. He reluctantly agreed to fight for his country and was shipped to France in the spring of 1918.

That fall, York's division was sent to support the Meus Argonne offensive. On October 8th, Corporal York and sixteen other soldiers were on a predawn mission under the command of Sergeant Bernard Early. Their mission was to seize the railroad near Chatel-Chehery. Following a map that was printed in French instead of English, they got lost and found themselves behind enemy lines. York and his fellow soldiers exchanged fire with the much larger German force—and within minutes, the Germans surprised the Americans by surrendering! The enemy soldiers had mistakenly thought themselves outnumbered.

Soon, the Germans realized they had surrendered too soon, and some machine gunners on a nearby ridge opened fire on the Americans. Alvin looked around and saw his fellow soldiers scream and crumple to the ground, riddled by machine-gun fire. York's best friend in the army, Murray Savage, lay dying a few yards away. Sergeant Early lay mortally wounded, bleeding profusely from three bullet wounds.

Two corporals took charge and ordered York to go up the ridge and silence the machine gun. In his journal, Alvin York recalled what happened next:

As soon as the machine guns opened fire on me, I began to exchange shots with them. There were over thirty German soldiers in the machinegun nest, keeping the gun firing continuously, and all I could do was touch the Germans off just as fast as I could. I was sharpshooting. I don't think I missed a shot. It was no time to miss.

In order to sight me or to swing their machine guns on me, the Germans had to show their heads above the trench, and every time I saw a head I just touched it off. All the time I kept yelling at them to come down. I didn't want to kill any more than I had to. But it was they or I. And I was giving them the best I had. Suddenly a German officer and five men jumped out of the trench and charged me with fixed bayonets. I changed to the old automatic and touched them off too. I touched off the sixth man first, then the fifth, then the fourth, then the third and so on. I wanted them to keep coming.

I got hold of the German major, and he told me if I wouldn't kill any more of them, he would make them quit firing. So, I told him all right if he would do it now. He blew a little whistle, and they quit shooting and came down and gave up.[4]

By the time the smoke had cleared, Alvin York and the nine remaining men in his unit had captured 132 German prisoners. For his heroism under fire, York was awarded the Congressional Medal of Honor. [5]

Why did I tell you this story? Because Alvin C. York reminds me so much of Shamgar. Alvin *started where he was*—the little Podunk town of Pall Mall, Tennessee. He *used what he had*—an amazing ability to shoot the eye out of a turkey or "touch off" a German machine gunner. He *did what he could*—walking right into a squad of German soldiers who were charging at him with fixed bayonets.

You see, I know that some people think that the story of Shamgar is nothing more than a wild myth. After all, how could one man defeat 600 sword wielding Philistines when he was armed with only a sharpened pole? How could one man overcome 600-to-one odds and save his entire nation from destruction? But is the story of Shamgar really so hard to believe?

I don't want you to think that in telling either the story of Shamgar or the story of Alvin York, I'm glorifying killing or war. I believe that war is an evil thing—but sometimes it's a necessary evil. I say this as a father who had two sons who served in the U.S. Marine Corps, one of whom fought in Iraq.

I see both Alvin York and Shamgar as reluctant warriors—men who took no pleasure in killing, but who fought in a just cause to save innocent lives. More importantly, I believe that the story of Shamgar has a great deal to teach us about how we can live a more effective and meaningful life.

Ultimately, the only way to find meaning in life is to live a life that counts for God—a life like that of Shamgar.

Shamgar started where he was—out on a farm in Palestine. He never got to go to one of the big universities in Alexandria, Damascus, or Nineveh. He never got to study battlefield tactics in one of the great military academies of Babylon or Assyria. He was a simple farmer who used a pair of oxen to plow his fields on a ranch outside of West Overshoe, just over the hill from Box Springs.

The Sacred NOW

Wherever "here" is, that's where you've got to start. If you're in Paris, Texas, there's no point in saying, "I want to start in Paris, France." If you have a dream or a calling to fulfill, don't wait until you can get to the Big City. Start building now, right where you are. Start planning, creating, and preparing.

THE POWER OF ONE

When is the best time to plant a fruit tree? Twenty years ago! But when is the second-best time? Right now! You can't undo yesterday, but you can begin again today.

People often think, "Someday, when I have more time, I'm going to make my dreams come true," or "Someday when I get off this farm and move to the big city, I'm going to accomplish great things." If that had been Shamgar's attitude, the Jewish people would all be speaking Philistine today.

Shamgar didn't think, "I'll defend Israel from the Philistines *someday*—maybe when I can find someone to go with me, or when I have saved up enough to buy a bigger ox goad." Shamgar didn't wait for "someday." He picked up his ox goad and got right to it. He started where he was, and he started at that very moment.

There is no telling how much more effective and successful you and I could be if we could grasp the importance of the Sacred Now, this very moment of time that is, and that will never be again. Yet Shamgar understood it well. He lived in the Sacred Now. He acted in the Sacred Now. He refused to waste the Sacred Now.

What do you want to do someday? Don't wait. Start now. Don't put off living. Live now. How do you want to be remembered after you're gone? How do you want your obituary to read? Well, here's a sobering thought: You are writing your obituary right now. Think of all the things you want people to read about your life when you're gone. Those are the things you need to be doing right now, while you're still here. As playwright George Bernard Shaw once observed, "If you take too long in deciding what to do with your life, you'll find you've already done it."

We may have stopped believing in Santa Claus and the Tooth Fairy, but most of us still believe in a far more ridiculous myth—the myth of "When I get more time." As in, "When I get more time, I'm going to write that novel." Or "When I get more time, I'm going to start my own business." Or "When I get more time, I'm going to volunteer at the local homeless shelter."

Why do you think you're ever going to have more time than you have right now? Does that bestselling novelist you applaud, that successful entrepreneur you envy, those selfless volunteers you admire have one more minute in their days than you do?

If you're waiting until you get more time, you have a long wait ahead of you. If you want to get anything accomplished before you die, then you must start here and start now. Don't "find time"—*make* time. That means you have to prioritize. You have to quit doing what doesn't count and start doing the very thing that is most important to you. And you must *do it now*.

John C. Maxwell told me of a man he once heard about—a man who, at the age of 55, had learned the true value of time. One day, this man sat down and did the math. Assuming a life span of 75 years and 52 weeks in

THE POWER OF ONE

a year, he punched these numbers into his calculator: 75 x 52 = 3,900.

What did that tell him? It told him that, in an average lifetime, he could expect to have 3,900 Saturdays to do with as he pleased. He could work on those Saturdays to make extra money, or he could use them to do some project he had always wanted to do, or he could enjoy those Saturdays with his family.

Then it hit him: "I'm 55 years old! I've already used up most of those 3,900 Saturdays!" Again, he tapped some numbers into his calculator, whereupon he discovered that over 2,800 of his lifetime allotment of Saturdays had already been used up! He had only a thousand or so Saturdays left to spend! He decided he had better use them wisely.

This man went out and bought a thousand marbles, one for every Saturday he had left, assuming a normal life span. He put the marbles in a clear plastic jar in his den. Then, every Saturday morning, he took one marble out of the jar and tossed it in the trash. He found that, week by week, as he watched the marbles diminish, he was able to focus his mind on the things that truly mattered in life. He could see his life draining out of that jar like sand falling through an hourglass— and that visual reminder of the brevity of life motivated him to get the priorities of his life in proper order.

I once heard a pastor observe, "Don't be paralyzed by the past nor hypnotized by the future. Stay riveted on the present moment. It's the key to your success."

As sales and marketing guru, Paul J. Meyer, once said, "Most time is wasted not in hours but in minutes. A bucket with a small hole in the bottom gets just as empty as a bucket that is deliberately poured out." And automaker Henry Ford once observed, "Most people get ahead during the time that others waste." It's true: Your time is your life. When you waste time, you waste a piece of your life.

According to an ancient Jewish legend, King Solomon once had his goldsmith fashion a ring and inscribe the band with words that would be fitting for all occasions and situations. The goldsmith did as the king directed. He created a beautiful golden ring and presented it to King Solomon. The king took the ring and examined the inscription on the band. It read: "This, too, shall pass."

King Solomon was baffled by the inscription, but he admired the ring and wore it every day. Some days were bad days, full of troubling news and woe. He might have to send out troops to battle Hittite raiders on the border or settle an argument between two of the concubines in his harem. On such days, he would read the inscription on his ring— "This, too, shall pass"—and be comforted.

THE POWER OF ONE

On other days, he would get news that a rich vein of gold had just been struck in one of his mines, or he would get a visit from that gorgeous Queen of Sheba, and he'd think, "Life doesn't get much better than this!" Just then, he would notice the inscription on his ring— "This, too, shall pass"—and he'd be sobered.

That ring truly did fit every occasion, and the inscription kept his mind focused on the fact that nothing lasts forever—neither bad times, nor good. The important thing was to make the most of whatever time he had, because "This, too, shall pass."

This very moment that you now inhabit is sacred moment, the Sacred Now. It is a holy gift entrusted to you by God. This moment, this heartbeat, is in your hands, and you may do with it what you will— but once it is spent, you will never get it back.

Granted, there are many things we must do to maintain our lives and take care of our families. But is it true that you couldn't find one hour out of twenty-four to devote to that project or goal or dream that you have been putting off? You couldn't spend one less hour front of the television or the computer? You couldn't skip one lunch hour or get up one hour earlier in the morning?

Someone once said, "Most of us spend our lives as if we had another one in the bank." Is that the way you've been living your life? Have you been letting life slip away from you as you marked time, killed time, wasted time? Every second of your life is irreversible. Every heartbeat is irreplaceable. Every Sacred Now is an opportunity that, once lost, will never come again.

Neil Armstrong, the first human being to set foot on the moon, wisely said, "I believe every human has a finite number of heartbeats. I don't intend to waste any of mine." And poet Carl Sandburg observed, "Time is the coin of your life. It is the only coin you have, and only you can determine how it will be spent. Be careful, lest you let other people spend it for you."

What are you trying to accomplish? What is your dream, your grand goal in life? Whatever that dream may be, you can achieve it, even if the odds are 600-to-one against it. Like Shamgar, you can beat the odds, overcome the obstacles, and win. Look, I know what you're up against because I've been there. You're facing a challenge that seems too big for you. People are telling you to give up on your goals, to let go of your dreams, to "face reality." You're beginning to think that maybe they're right, maybe you should give up and find something safer to do—something less risky.

Don't think of quitting for a moment, my friend! Don't you dare give up—at least not until you've finished this book! What do you want to accomplish? What is your impossible dream? Do you aspire to write the Great American Novel? Start your own business? Rescue homeless children from the streets of Calcutta or Buenos Aires or inner-city Los Angeles? Run for public office? Find a cure for cancer, AIDS, or Alzheimer's disease? Be the first man or woman on Mars?

You realize, of course, that the odds are against you—a 600-to-one shot, at least. But so what? Other people, just like you, have beaten those odds and have achieved great things. They have hammered dreams into reality. Shamgar did it. Why shouldn't you?

What if the whole world bets against you? What does it matter that your family and friends say you don't stand a chance? By the time you finish this book, you'll know something they don't. You'll know the three success secrets of Shamgar. You'll know how to beat those 600-to-one odds—and win.

THREE

The Power of One

– Jay Strack

*"What, then, shall we say in response to these things?
If God is for us, who can be against us?"*
Romans 8:31

What kind of chaos would occur if America's stop signs, warning signs, and traffic lights in our transportation system were suddenly removed? There would be death, fear, and loss beyond imagination.

That is what happened to two teens outside of Tampa, Florida a few years ago. They died at the hands of pranksters who thought it would be fun to steal traffic signs. Driving home after an innocent night of bowling with friends was their last.

One person can make a difference that will damage lives or influence for good. The habit we want to develop is thinking through and making choices that will live on to instill good in others.

What would life be like in a world without warning signs? How many would make decisions that create life-altering shame and guilt? This culture is very close to substituting all stop signs with a "Yield" sign – do as you please as long as no one is looking. Broken families, destroyed lives, and death by overdose are daily news.

Shamgar lived in a civilization without stop signs, order, or justice, similar to what we see happening in America. Twice in the book of Judges—in Judges 17:6 and 21:25—we read this bleak description of the days: *"In those days Israel had no king; everyone did as they saw fit."* There was no king in Israel—no law, justice, or standard of right and wrong. Three thousand years later, people still choose to do what is right in their own eyes. We live in a world of blinding lights, distorted value lines, and shattered promises that have created multiple norms and the inability to see right and wrong in reality. The expression "no absolutes" dominates news, entertainment, media, legal cases, and education. Instead of traditional Biblical morality, we have moral relativism. With no ultimate truth in our lives, choices are instead made by emotions.[5]

The words "inclusion and equity" are often used in ways that cause separation rather than unconditional love. The dictionary defines being "included" as "being part of the whole" and "equity" as "fair and impartial." What we see happening in the culture is the opposite. Both words can correctly be defined through the Great Commandment in Matthew –22:37-39: *"Jesus replied: Love the Lord your God with all your heart and with all your soul and with all your mind. This is the first and greatest commandment. And the second is like it: 'Love your neighbor as yourself."*

Labels are not a part of loving your neighbor. As Christians, we will continue the practice of inclusion of persons as long as we live on the earth, but not the inclusion of sin as defined in the Scriptures. A demand of respect for immoral choices cannot be given.

Our belief is a simple one: *"God created mankind in his own image, in the image of God he created them; male and female He created them."* (Genesis 1:27)

A percentage of our culture has adopted the slogan, "No rules, do what feels good, just have fun." Every addict I have ever known, including myself, has excused sin by saying, "Leave me alone. I am not hurting anyone. It's my life." But the truth is that we cannot stop our choices from affecting others. What we do ends up living on in the lives of those we influence through word, deed, or the lack of. We may be separated from Shamgar by half a world and millenniums, but we have something in common with his circumstances. Like Shamgar, our moral and social standards break down when people do what is "right in their own eyes."

Our world needs men and women like Shamgar who are willing to step into the moral vacuum and choose to do what is right and righteous. As my good friend and brother, Dr. Jack Graham says, "It is never right to do wrong and never wrong to do right." I like simple statements that pack a powerful, no further discussion punch like that one.

The history of ancient Israel, as recorded in the Old Testament, is the history of a nation that sank into moral and spiritual chaos, accompanied by social breakdown and desolation. Could America be headed for the same destination?

America has projected a normalization of immorality. It is the reason that Student Leadership University teaches that every person must have personal ownership of a Biblical worldview. It cannot be mom or dad's faith; it must be confidently your own. Proverbs 14:12 tells us, *"There is a way that appears to be right, but in the end, it leads to death."* These are times that cry out for people to take a stand where they are, to use what they have, and to do what they can. That includes a sure Biblical worldview, a knowledge and understanding of Scripture, and a consistent prayer life.
It was not uncommon, during the time of Shamgar, for the Israelites to follow the worship of the pagan gods as the non-Israelites did. The plethora of the surrounding cultural habits drew them in as they stopped praising the one true God of Israel. Some turned to Moloch, the brass fire god to whom children were horribly sacrificed, or to Baal, a god of the Canaanites.[6]

By turning to alien gods, the people of ancient Israel removed themselves from the guidance and protection of the One True God Who delivered their forefathers from slavery in Egypt.

What we know about life is that it is made up of a series of choices and decisions. The importance of who you listen to is evident. I can't stress it enough – Know what you believe and Whom you believe in. That is why SLU values experiential learning through "the books you read, the places you go, the people you meet, and the Scripture you memorize." We created SLU 101 in Orlando and San Antonio; SLU 201 in Washington, D.C.; SLU 301 throughout Europe; and SLU 401 in Israel and Jordan. On our Paris-Normandy trips, I usually make my way to the Sculpture Gardens of the Musee Rodin Gardens and meditate in between waiting on groups of students to arrive. We have sessions as we walk among the various sculpture gardens – The Thinker, The Gates of Hell, and the Monument to the Burghers of Calais.

One warm day in June I was doing just that when shouting erupted, "La Main de Dieu, the hand of God is missing!" I was confused. Was she referring to Rodin's famous sculpture, "The Hand of God?" The clarification came through the BBC story of the sculpture theft at the Museum of Fine Arts in Buenos Aires, Argentina.[7] Sculpted by the French master Auguste Rodin in 1898, the work depicts a hand molding a diminutive human form. It symbolically portrays how God's hand shapes and fashions our lives. The newspaper headlines in Buenos Aires announced, "The Hand of God is Missing!" People asked each other, "Where is 'The Hand of God"?

I keep a plaster model of the work on my desk and often contemplate the question myself. War and hatred seem to rule the globe, and anxiety and fear fill hearts over the "might be's." Worldwide, the question is being asked, "Where is the Hand of God?" The more I consider the question, the more firmly I believe that the hand of God is poised and waiting to bless those who choose righteousness as the mission and purpose of life.

In the days of Shamgar, the Israelites as a people gave up on hope and opened the door to depression and the mental slavery the enemy poured upon them. Poverty was the "norm" in those days, and the enemy wanted them to believe that it would always be this way as a tool of subjugation. Many, especially the next generation, were asking, "Where is the Hand of the God of the Jews?"

Shamgar stepped into this moral vacuum and accepted the challenge of saving his nation from the invading hordes of Philistine terrorists. Knowing the sins of the culture and feeling the oppression of poverty, Shamgar believed his resource to be the hand of God. He thought that starting where he was, out on his farm, using what he had, and doing what he could was enough if the Faithful God came through to forgive Israel. And He did just that.

Shamgar spent many a day preparing for this battle. He thought out strategy, best-case scenario, and worst-case. It is a good plan for any of us, any day.

As you read this, I hope you are convinced that the enemy of our souls is not meant to rule us. Breathe in the courage of Shamgar and begin to prepare for the battle ahead.

In 2 Timothy 4:2, the apostle Paul issues this challenge: *"be prepared in season and out of season; correct, rebuke and encourage—with great patience and careful instruction."* I like how this is expressed in the King James Version: *"Be instant in season, out of season."* Be instant! Be ready right now! To be instant is to be focused, eyes fixed on the goal, regardless of whether the conditions around us are favorable or unfavorable. Be instantly ready and prepared to seize opportunity, meet the challenge, and respond to every threat without fear.

To be instant, in the original Greek language that Paul uses, means "to be steady, ready, and at hand." The mental picture Paul suggests is that of a soldier with his hand resting on the hilt of his sword. His sword isn't drawn yet—but he's ready, instant, prepared to respond to changing conditions and unexpected events.[8] The Lord is calling you and me to be prepared to give our all to any opportunity, whether in times of great prosperity or harsh adversity.

One phrase Paul uses— "in season, out of season"—is more significant than it seems at first glance. The Greek word that is translated as "season" is derived from the Greek word for "opportunity." It is the same word that is used in Luke 4:13, in the story of Satan's temptation of Jesus in the wilderness. This verse tells us, *"When the devil had finished all this tempting, he left Him until an opportune time."*— When Paul writes that we should be "instant in season, out of season," he tells us to be alert to those opportune moments. You may already be experiencing them.

The apostle Paul didn't just preach—he practiced and displayed what he preached. Do you know where he was when he wrote, *"Be instant in season, out of season"?* He was in chains, locked in a Roman prison for the second time.

God used Paul in mighty ways from the day of his salvation until his death and every day forward as his journals are read in the Scripture. The apostle preached and founded churches around the eastern Mediterranean Sea and throughout the region. He debated the great philosophers of Athens. He met with Peter and James and helped shape the church's future for the centuries to come. He wrote inspired treatises on theology and Christian living, such as his letters to the Romans,

THE POWER OF ONE

Corinthians, and Thessalonians, which are included in the sacred canon of the Holy Scripture, the Word of God.

Suddenly, those days of travel were over. Instead, Paul was confined to one dark cave, where misery was his cellmate. We know that he received visitors, and he witnessed to the Praetorium guards and other prisoners who came and went. All the while, he remained suffering in chains. Imagine with me the worst—being held against your will by an enemy. Yet here is Paul, able to write words of encouragement because he had prepared for *"in season and out of season."*

I have visited this dark, musty place on several occasions, and I can tell you that even cleaned up to tourism standards, it is a gloomy, hopeless stone hole without windows of any kind. Paul, the prisoner of Nero and the great Roman Empire, planted churches, spoke before government officials, and told the story of Christ intersecting his life. In Paul's day, a rabbi was trained to recite daily the gratitude for one's station in life through the negative statements: "Thank you that I am not a Gentile or a slave." Paul gave up his status as a prominent Jew, a highly esteemed Roman citizen, and his reputation as one of the most educated men in the known world. He did it to obey the call of God to go to the Gentiles, a practice that was against all that he had lived by. Along the way, he was persecuted, criticized, thrown out of towns, endured shipwrecks, and multiple imprisonments.

If anyone had the right to "give up," it was Paul. Instead, he used what he had – an astounding testimony of an intersection by the living Savior, a quill, and a parchment, either brought by visitors or granted to him by the Romans. At first thought, it seems like meager resources. But as the darkness grew in the cave, so did the light within Paul. He wrote the words of light we are privileged to read, memorize, and receive wisdom, understanding, and encouragement from. What may have looked like a useless effort, one man journaling in his gloomy prison has lived on to transform lives and bring glory to the name of Jesus for millenniums. Never measure your work only by what you see in the present, for *"God can do anything, you know..."*

Paul chose to start where he was, use what he had, and do what he could. While in prison, he wrote some of his most famous and influential letters—Colossians, Philemon, Ephesians, Philippians, and, near the end of his life, 1 and 2 Timothy. Those letters are, in places, poignant and painful to read. Again and again, we read such lines as, *"Remember my chains,"* and *"I am an ambassador in chains. Pray that I may declare [the Gospel] fearlessly, as I should;" "What has happened to me has really served to advance the gospel."*

Paul understood his calling and that God could use his life anywhere, at any time. He wasn't a quitter or an opportunist; he was just totally given over to God's will. Paul could not have imagined his influence would go on for generation after generation. In front of him was hopeless darkness, but he refused to believe only in what could be seen. You may never know the influence you have on others. Charlie wasn't there the night I gave my life to Jesus, but his prayers were.

Opportunity: Grab it or Lose it

As the Power of One, we use what we have and trust God to multiply the increase. Paul lived "in and out of season" but always looking for opportunities to influence beyond his physical geography. My favorite definition of "opportunity" is a "wind that blows favorably." The Greek word for opportunity suggests the image of sails billowing at full mast on a great ship, clipping along at top speed toward its destination. Dynamic momentum comes to mind. If we are instant and alert to the opportunities in front of us, we will be like ships with unfurled sails, ready to catch the following favorable wind of opportunity.

Tragically, most people are like ships at anchor, with their sails furled, masts bare, and dead in the water. The winds of opportunity blow past them, and vessels continue to sit still at anchor, their hulls collecting barnacles. By contrast, Shamgar was a ship that was going places, a ship that was simply unstoppable.

The Greek sculptor Lysippus lived four centuries before Christ and is credited with more than 1,500 statues and artistic works. Renowned for the delicacy of detail in his statues, Lysippus is considered one of the first sculptors to focus on the detailed hair rendering in his subjects.[9] He worked in bronze and modeled his statues after heroes, athletes, and the Greek gods. He was also the portrait sculptor of Alexander the Great.[10] Imagine that opportunity!

I learned of his works when I first encountered his inspirational "Kairos," the Greek word for Opportunity. With careful detail, he sculpted a powerful, symbolic image of the timeline of Opportunity: a brawny figure with wings on his feet and a huge lock of hair flowing from his forehead. The realistic muscles, veins, and facial characteristics are impressive from the front. The view from the back is the opposite: a completely bald head and a flabby, wrinkled body. What do you imagine the sculptor meant to convey?

After studying extensive notes and researching this sculpture, I have come to believe that the winged feet symbolize a swiftly moving Opportunity that won't be here long. The lock of hair on Opportunity's forehead is given as a tool to keep Opportunity from slipping away. The baldness of the back of Opportunity's head tells us that once it has passed you by, you may never reach for it again.

Although Shamgar never saw the statue of Lysippus, he clearly understood the powerful truths it conveyed. He knew opportunities must be grabbed as they come within reach, or they would be lost. He

THE POWER OF ONE

looked around and saw that the roads and highways of his nation were deserted; his neighbors were cowering in fear, and bands of terrorists roamed across the land of the Jews without hindrance. Much like the terrorist activity of our day, fear of impending crisis ruled the air. In Shamgar's mind, the dire situation gave birth to an opportunity knocking on his door.

If you are reading this and say, "I just don't see any opportunity ahead. How can I be prepared?" I answer, "Do just as Shamgar did. If you can't see an opportunity, get up and make an opportunity."

My friend Pat Williams used to tell me about the thrill of watching one of his players seize an opportunity to make a clutch shot in an NBA game—and about the crushing disappointment when a player lets that Opportunity slip by. Games and entire championships have been decided because a player either took or passed up an opportunity that lasted as briefly as two or three-tenths of a second. An instant of hesitation can cost you the game and subject you to years of regret because every Opportunity has a shot clock.

In your own life, you may have only minutes, seconds, or even a fraction of a second to:

- Turn the wheel and slam on the brakes in time to save precious life.
- Make the most important decision of your career.

- Speak a word of hope to someone who is considering suicide.
- Introduce yourself to the person who could become the love of your life.
- Say "I love you" to someone you may never see again.
- Share the message of God's grace and forgiveness with a lost and hurting soul.

Horatio Nelson is regarded as the most outstanding officer in the Royal Navy's history. His reputation is based on a series of remarkable victories, culminating in the Battle of Trafalgar, where he was killed in his moment of triumph. The poet Byron referred to him as "Britannia's God of War." He declared, "Time is everything; five minutes make the difference between victory and defeat."[11]

Be alert, be instant, be prepared. Seize the opportunity as it approaches.

The Reality of the Enemy

Hesitation often comes in the form of doubt and lack of confidence in yourself and in the Creator God. We do have a real enemy who does not want us to succeed in our lives. His name is Satan, and he is defined in The Book as the devil, adversary, enemy, father of lies, ruler of demons, evil one, murderer, ruler of this world, and more. He would like nothing better than to dull our senses and make us lazy and inattentive so that he can steal away opportunities. This is the satanic strategy for neutralizing and hindering us from reaching our full potential for the Kingdom of God.

In his timeless work, *The Screwtape Letters*, C. S. Lewis depicts a senior devil named Screwtape who writes letters of advice to a junior devil, his nephew Wormwood. This junior devil is trying to use his wiles to neutralize a young Christian. Screwtape offers this evil advice: "The great thing is to prevent his doing anything. As long as he does not convert it into action, it does not matter how much he thinks about this new repentance. Let the little brute wallow in it. Let him do anything but act. No amount of piety in his imagination and affections will harm us if we can keep it out of his will."[12]

Lewis is speaking of what happens when we get caught but don't repent fully; it's like stalling out a car or using the vague word "someday." 1 John 1:9 says, *"If we confess our sins, he is faithful and just and will forgive us our sins and purify us from all unrighteousness."* The word "confess" here means "to say the same thing as another, i.e. to agree with."[13]

Until we hate our sin as God does and see it as He sees it, we will never be set free from the habit that holds us captive. We might cry and tell everyone we are sorry, but we are stuck in Neverland until we hate the sin and its hold over us to the point that it is sickening to our very souls.

Beliefs are truly owned once they are put into action. Note to self: Decide today to make the most of every opportunity. Whether we work in an office or in the home, in the classroom or traveling about, whether we are in prison like Paul or in a field behind a pair of oxen like Shamgar, let us declare to live out God's call for us.

Legacy Lives and Breathes

When I think of the good that was born out of Paul's imprisonment, it reminds me of the captivity of the Russian novelist and historian Alexander Solzhenitsyn. As an ADD student, I was forced to take Russian Literature in college to satisfy my deficient language requirements. I thought it would be one of the most boring times of my life. Instead, one fascinating story of Solzhenitsyn motivated me to graduate Cum Laude from Charleston Southern University in under three years.

In 1945, Solzhenitsyn was sentenced without the benefit of a trial to eight years of hard labor in the gulags—the Soviet forced labor camps that were used primarily to imprison political dissidents. His crime: Solzhenitsyn had criticized Soviet dictator Joseph Stalin in a private letter to a school friend (the Soviets censored everything in those days, including the mail). At the time of his arrest, Solzhenitsyn was a committed Marxist and had served with distinction in World War II as an artillery captain in the Soviet army. None of that mattered to the judge who sentenced him to hard labor.

Five years into the sentence, Solzhenitsyn was sent to a prison camp in Kazakhstan, where he developed a cancerous tumor. He was operated on by doctors at the camp hospital and then moved to a surgical ward where he wrote the famed The Gulag Archipelago.

"Following an operation, I am lying in the surgical ward of a camp hospital. I cannot move. I am hot and feverish, but nonetheless, my thoughts do not dissolve into delirium, and I am grateful to Dr. Boris Nikolayevich Kornfeld, who is sitting beside my cot and talking to me all evening about his life. The light has been turned out, so it will not hurt my eyes. There is no one else in the ward. Fervently, he tells me the long story of his conversion to Christianity. I am astonished at the conviction of the new convert, at the ardor of his words."[14]

It seems after Kornfeld had given years of faithful service to the Communist political leader, Joseph Stalin, the dictator turned on Kornfeld, had him arrested, and sent him to the gulag system of labor camps in the Soviet Union, from which many people were never again seen.

Dr. Kornfeld spoke about his past sins and how he deserved nothing but punishment—yet God had sent

Jesus to die in his place and save him from his sins. Solzhenitsyn would later say that he sensed "such mystical knowledge" in Kornfeld's voice that he trembled in his cot. After Dr. Kornfeld finished his story, he got up, went into the next room, lay down on a cot, and went to sleep. A while later, Solzhenitsyn also drifted off to sleep. He was awakened at dawn by voices and the sound of footsteps in the corridor. Hospital orderlies were carrying Kornfeld's limp body to the operating room. During the night, someone had crept into the hospital and hammered his skull with a mallet as he slept. Dr. Kornfeld died on the operating table, having never regained consciousness.

Solzhenitsyn was profoundly affected by the fact that the last words the doctor had ever spoken were the words he said at Solzhenitsyn's bedside—the story of his life-changing encounter with Jesus Christ. Dr. Kornfeld's words would continue to haunt Solzhenitsyn over the next few months.

His surgery was unsuccessful, and Solzhenitsyn's condition worsened. In 1953, he was sent to a cancer clinic, where he received radiation treatment and was cured. He later told biographer Joseph Pearce (author of Solzhenitsyn: A Soul in Exile) that after being stricken with cancer, then cleansed of it, "I came back to a deep awareness of God and a deep understanding of life." He believed God had spared his life for a purpose, so he committed to Jesus Christ.

THE POWER OF ONE

Kornfeld's prophetic words were his last words on earth, but as Solzhenitsyn later wrote, "those words lay upon me as an inheritance. You cannot brush off that kind of inheritance by shrugging your shoulders...."

Soon after his release from prison, Solzhenitsyn published several works that revealed the dehumanizing conditions faced by political dissidents in the Soviet Union, particularly in the labor camps. These were banned in the USSR but copied by hand and widely distributed throughout the literary underground. The KGB (the Soviet intelligence and internal security agency) tried to suppress his writings. Still, his work garnered so much worldwide acclaim—including the Nobel Prize for literature in 1970—that the Soviet authorities were afraid to move against him.

He lived in exile in Switzerland and the United States for twenty years. His writings—especially The Gulag Archipelago—are credited as one of several factors that directly led to the collapse of Soviet communism in 1991. After the fall of the Soviet Union, Solzhenitsyn returned to Russia, where he spoke out on the deepest needs of the Russian people. Their need, Solzhenitsyn said, was not political or economic. It was spiritual. The Russian people, he said in his last public appearance in Moscow, had lost "the ability to answer the principal problem of life and death. People are prepared to stuff their heads with anything and to talk of any subject, but only to block off the contemplation of this subject: the only solution to the problem of life and death is finding eternal life through Jesus Christ."

Looking ahead to his death, Solzhenitsyn said it would "be just a peaceful transition. As a Christian, I believe there is life after death."

Boris Kornfield has a small biography, but his last words were anointed by the Holy Spirit and used to light a fire of salvation and courage in Solzhenitsyn and, ultimately, the world. Like Kornfield, we may never know, at least on earth, what power our last words to a person under challenging circumstances might produce. Boris Kornfield is rejoicing in heaven over the stories of salvation that Solzhenitsyn carried on for him.

These men show us the power of one man's testimony. We know from history and personal experience that the work of God is multiplied when shared. Ask yourself, "Am I prepared today to use what I have to share my story?"

Like Shamgar and the apostle Paul, Solzhenitsyn started where he was—in prison. He used what he had—his memories of his sufferings and his ability to write about them with power and clarity. He did what he could—at significant personal risk, he told his story, and it changed the world.

Legacy lives on into the next generation. When we do it right, we leave an inheritance of wisdom, as Solzhenitsyn and the Apostle Paul did. When we do it wrong, its impact is unproductive and multiplies anger, fear, and even hatred to the next generation. We read seven times in the book of Judges that "the Israelites (again) did what was evil in the sight of the Lord," even after He had miraculously delivered them. As you read the chapters, one theme can be seen that is most probably attributed to this behavior: "they forgot the Lord their God and served the Baals and the Asherahs." (Judges 3:7). It frightens me to think how easily we mix worldview values and false gods together in our country. It may very well destroy us unless we remember the One True God this country was founded upon. His name is Faithful.

When you walk into my home, there is an 18-foot wall in the stairwell that displays a hand-painted, massive scroll with the words: *"Choose you this day whom you will serve, but as for me and my house, we will serve the Lord."* My wife and I chose that as the first décor of our new home three decades ago. We wanted our children to see the declaration each morning as they opened their bedroom door. As a family, we decided to continue the work God has called us to. Let it never be said of any of us who name Christ as Savior that we went back to the land of "before" God did a work in our lives. Instead, daily proclaim to live in the present land of "We will serve the Lord." (Josh 24:15)

You will read many narratives of history in this book. These are gifts. Listen, read, and think deeply.

Think Cumulatively

As a farmer in the hinterland of ancient days, Shamgar had no news media like CNN, Fox News Channel, or social media to inform him. We don't know for sure, but it's possible Shamgar farmed the uplands of southern Palestine, the same area where a wealthy man named Abraham once owned a vast cattle ranch. Shamgar could look out over the plains from the high, hilly land to the sea. His view showed the Philistines raiding the land of Israel from both land and sea.

The Philistines commonly used style attacks of small-scale strikes rather than massive incursions. By the time the Israelites could assemble and mobilize a fighting force to launch a counterattack, the Philistines would be gone, only to return later through a different entry. Watching these raids from a distance, hearing the stories of how his neighbors were being attacked, robbed, and slaughtered, Shamgar became outraged over the violence of the Philistines. I imagine he spent many a day and night thinking, "What could I do that others have not been able to do?" He was only one man, but Shamgar could no longer stand by in fear while the Philistines burned the fields of his neighbors and plundered his nation. Enough was enough!

When Shamgar decided to attack the Philistines, he had no assurance that his mission would succeed, at least not on the first try. Logic tells us that Shamgar did not kill all 600 at once. If he had, he would have gotten more than two verses! There would surely be an engraved rock or statue with his name on it.

Shamgar did what courageous, thoughtful, prepared leaders do; he counted the cost. Personally, his life would be in danger, but he could at least save one family, and they might join him in the battle. Perhaps his brave effort would multiply out to others in the Hebrew community. He thought cumulatively.

Shamgar also demonstrated an essential leadership principle: You can't be a leader tomorrow if you can't lead yourself today. It is useless to say, "Someday, I'm going to impact the world. Tomorrow, I'm going to make a difference." Authentic leaders don't dream big and then procrastinate. They gather wisdom, plan against the odds, prepare for challenges, and get it done. They understand the simple but often neglected truth that you can't begin from where you wish you were. Begin from where you are and move forward by faith.

You can't impact the world by wishing your circumstances, family, looks, or career are something they are not. Suppose you are a student, a pastor, an insurance salesman, a mom, or a farmer like Shamgar. In that case, you probably are not in a position to change the foreign policy of the United States of America, but you can still impact your circle of influence. You have one. We all do.

If you are a student, your actions and words can influence the students and teachers at your school. If you are a pastor, you can profoundly affect your community and congregation. If you are a salesman, you can help your clients make wise, essential decisions for the benefit of their families. If you are a teacher, you can impact the future through your classroom. If you are a parent, you can impact the next generation by raising healthy children. You can be the one to clear conflict with a calm spirit and offer appreciation and encouragement. Everyone can impact and influence if we choose to.

On one of our trips through Oxford with our SLU students, we were being led by a guide through the beautiful campuses and surrounding areas. Out of nowhere, a man began yelling, "You are a liar! Stop lying!" He repeated this over and over, coming closer to the group each time. Fear began to fall on the guide and our group. What could be done, the guide asked me. I walked up to the drunken man, put my arm around him and said, "Man, you don't want to do this. You are drunk. I know what that is like. Let's step over to the side and let me listen to your story." The man calmed within a moment, and we talked. When he explained his misunderstanding of what the guide was saying, I was able to share forgiveness, Jesus, and encourage him to think differently. Again, no boasting here. He could have just as easily hit me with his fist! Proverbs 15:1 says, "*A gentle answer turns away wrath, but a harsh*

THE POWER OF ONE

word stirs up anger." Think of how many situations God could have used you to be the "gentle answer."

Being a farmer, Shamgar understood the principle of multiplication: start with one plant and soon you have more. Planting one kernel of wheat in the ground will produce a stalk bearing up to three heads of grain. In each head are from 15 to 35 kernels of wheat. One kernel of wheat can easily make more than a hundred new kernels at harvest time. Plant a hundred kernels, and they will produce a hundred times a hundred kernels, or ten thousand. Those ten thousand kernels can yield a million new kernels, and so on! It all starts with a single kernel of wheat. It all starts with the Power of One.

One leader creates cumulative thinking when his or her thoughts and prayers multiply forth to all who hear, see, and experience their influence. There is no limit to what God can accomplish through you. There is no limit to the Power of One because there are no limits to the Power of *the* One who created you.

Many believe that human society runs on autopilot, steered and driven by forces beyond the influence of any individual human being. But we know better. Throughout human history, we read of people hindered by challenges or meager resources who profoundly affected the course of human events through sheer tenacity and bravery. The Power of One can influence many.

Professional tennis player Arthur Ashe was such a man. Ashe acquired HIV from a blood transfusion during heart bypass surgery. That tragedy inspired him to create the Arthur Ashe Foundation for the Defeat of AIDS and the Arthur Ashe Institute for Urban Health. He was posthumously awarded the Presidential Medal of Freedom for his servant leadership. This grand champion was the first black player selected to the United States Davis Cup team. He won three Grand Slam titles in singles and two in doubles and was the only black man ever to win the singles at Wimbledon, the US Open, and the Australian Open. Just because no one else had done it did not stop Ashe from trying. He wrote, "True heroism is remarkably sober, very undramatic. It is not the urge to surpass all others at whatever cost, but the urge to serve others at whatever cost."[15] His courage leaves a mark on history.

The power of one becomes cumulative thinking through leadership. President Ronald Reagan was just one man, but he believed in cumulative thinking. Even before he ran for President, he told friends and associates his simple plan for dealing with the Soviet Union. He planned to abandon the "détente" approach of previous presidents (endless rounds of diplomatic concessions, cultural contacts, and economic talks) in favor of a strategy he described in four words "We win, they lose."

When Reagan's foreign policy advisors heard his plan, they were aghast. They feared he would lead the

THE POWER OF ONE

nation into war. After all, American prestige and power were in decline, and the Soviets were advancing, having solidified their hold on Eastern Europe by taking over Afghanistan and establishing client states in Central and South America, right on America's doorstep. Most American foreign policy experts feared the USSR and urged Reagan to moderate his rhetoric to avoid angering the Russian bear.

Ignoring the timid advice of the diplomats, Reagan pursued his "We win, they lose" strategy for eight years. In the beginning, he was just one man with a vision for toppling the "evil empire" of the Soviet Union.[6] But Ronald Reagan was a cumulative thinker. He started as a lone opponent of Soviet expansionism, and soon he was joining forces with others who had the same vision of a world without an Iron Curtain: Pope John Paul II, Czech dissident Vaclav Havel, British Prime Minister Margaret Thatcher, Polish Solidarity leader Lech Walesa, and yes, Alexander Solzhenitsyn.

On June 12, 1987, Reagan went to Berlin's Brandenburg Gate and spoke those words that shook the foundations of the Soviet empire: "General Secretary Gorbachev, if you seek peace, if you seek prosperity for the Soviet Union and Eastern Europe, if you seek liberalization, come here to this gate! Mr. Gorbachev, open this gate! Mr. Gorbachev, tear down this wall!"

The Berlin Wall was opened by East Germans on November 9, 1989, and torn down by the end of 1990. I have been to the spot where the wall once stood, amazed that such a vast change could occur through one man's vision. The Supreme Soviet officially dissolved the USSR, and the Soviet Union passed into history, just as Ronald Reagan had predicted it would before he even ran for president: "We win, they lose."[16] That's the power of one. That's the power of cumulative thinking.

You don't have to be rich, powerful, or famous to positively impact your world. You just need to jump in and try. History has shown that you plus the courage given by God upon request are always enough.

FOUR

Your Ox Goad

- Pat Williams

"Being the best at whatever talent you have; that's what stimulates life." Coach Tom Landry

What a difference thirty centuries can make. Shamgar's job would have been much easier if he could have faced all of those Philistines from the turret of an M1 Abrams battle tank or from the cockpit of a Blackhawk helicopter armed with 7.62 mm machine guns. But he didn't have that kind of firepower at his disposal. All he had was an ox goad. That's it. Just a long wooden pole. Shamgar's resources were limited, to say the least. But he took his limited resources and offered them entirely to God. He used what he had.

Why didn't Shamgar have a sword, shield, or helmet? Two reasons: Because he wasn't a professional soldier and because the enemy prohibited weapons for the people of Israel. They kept the people impoverished and weak with the lack of basic necessities. Shamgar was a man of the soil, not a man of war. When the Philistines swarmed into Israel and stalked his land,

Shamgar had to face them with nothing in his fist but a long-sharpened stick. In the hands of Shamgar, however, that spindly stick became as lethal as a Tomahawk cruise missile.

Shamgar was the third in a series of judges who God raised to lead the nation of Israel between the deaths of Joshua and the rise of King Saul. The judges of Israel were not formally recognized leaders. They were not elected, appointed, anointed, or installed. Israel had no formal leadership whatsoever. "In those days," the book of Judges tells us, "There was no king in Israel, but every man did that which was right in his own eyes."

And what the people thought was right in their own eyes was horribly wrong in the eyes of God. The people fell away from God and his Law. They began worshipping the demon gods of the surrounding culture. Their society began to crumble and decay, and in time, they were taken captive by neighboring nations. While in captivity, the people would repent and return to God, and God would raise up a new leader, a judge, a person with enormous natural leadership abilities. That judge would then deliver the people from their bondage.

The first of these judges was Othniel, who victoriously led an army of Israelites against the Mesopotamians. The second judge was Ehud, whose army killed 10,000 soldiers of Moab. But Shamgar, the third judge, differs significantly from Othniel and Ehud. He does not lead an army—he is an army of one. He

THE POWER OF ONE

faces a hopeless situation—and he faces it alone and friendless.

Why was Shamgar alone? Perhaps it was because he couldn't get anyone to join him. I suspect the nation had sunk into such moral decline that there simply wasn't a man within miles with the courage to stand with Shamgar and guard his back.

Then again, it's possible that Shamgar simply preferred to work alone. He may have decided that none of his neighbors had the stealth, strength, courage, or physical prowess to fight a vastly superior enemy like the Philistines. He may have decided that his chances were better if he acted alone than if he relied on the dubious "help" of his neighbors. Whatever the reason, we know that Shamgar fought alone, armed only with an ox goad.

Why an ox goad? There must have been a better weapon available than a pointed wooden pole! An ox goad may have been the closest thing to a weapon anyone in Israel had at the time. The nation had fallen into such a state of moral and social decline that the arts of the weapon—the smith and the blacksmith—had been lost. No one in Israel knew how to make a proper weapon anymore.

There were, after all, similar times in Israel's history. For example, about four centuries after Shamgar, in the early days of King Saul, identical conditions prevailed. The book of 1 Samuel records that not a blacksmith could be found in the whole land of Israel because the Philistines had said, "Otherwise, the Hebrews will make swords or spears!" All Israel had no choice but to go to the Philistines to have their plow shares, mattocks, axes, and sickles sharpened. The price was two-thirds of a shekel for sharpening plowshares and mattocks and a third for pointing forks, axes, and repointing goads. On the day of the battle, not a soldier with Saul and Jonathan had a sword or spear in his hand; only Saul and his son Jonathan had them.

The nation had sunk so low that it was at the mercy of its enemies to obtain any weapons of protection or defense in battle. Such a nation places itself at the mercy of its enemies and puts itself at serious risk of extinction. That is the condition of Israel in the days of Shamgar. The people had such a complete lack of national pride and self-respect that they had abdicated their duty to defend themselves, their families, and their land against foreign invaders. Not a sword or a shield could be found throughout the land of Israel, not even a spear or a dagger. The closest thing in the whole country to a weapon of any kind was a farmer's ox goad.

The impression we get of those times is that Israel consisted of a vast Silent Majority. The people all knew that the Philistines were invading their land, killing, robbing, and raping their people, so they said, "Somebody ought to do something about this! Somebody ought to call out the army, call out the Marines! Why doesn't Somebody do something?" No

THE POWER OF ONE

one in the entire country would say, "I'll step up, I'll take responsibility." No one would say that—Until Shamgar stepped forward.

Seven Resources You Already Have

Did the people look up to Shamgar as a leader? No. He was just a farmer like the rest of them. Shamgar was recognized as a hero and a judge of Israel when he achieved his fantastic victory over the Philistines. Perhaps he floated the idea of defense, and others scoffed. It was a grim situation.

The Philistine terrorists roamed Israel, killing entire families, taking what they wanted, and operating without opposition. We are told that the situation was so bad that "the roads were abandoned; travelers took to winding paths" (Judg. 5:6). The people abandoned the roads and the villages. They huddled in fear out in the wilderness, praying their enemies wouldn't find them. In all of Israel, only Shamgar dared to take up an ox goad and make a bold stand at the bloody crossroads of history.

Shamgar started where he was, and he used what he had. He picked up his ox goad and went to war. You may say, "But my resources are so limited that I can't afford an ox goad! I'm willing to start where I am—but with what? I don't have anything at all to take into battle!

My friend, you have more resources than you can imagine. Even if you don't have a sharp stick, you have a powerful arsenal of resources. Offer those resources to

God, and you will be amazed at what he chooses to accomplish through you.

If you are willing to start where you are, use what you have, and do what you can, then you can become a hero like Shamgar. But if you refuse to use the resources God has given you, then you are no better off than Shamgar's cowardly neighbors, who huddled in the wilderness, afraid of the open roads, scared of their own shadows.

What is your ox goad? What do you have to work with? I want to suggest seven possessions that God has given you— seven powerful resources you can use to become a person of action like Shamgar. I'm sure you have many more resources than the ones I am about to list, but I have no doubt that you at least have these seven below.

These are your ox goads. After I have listed them for you, pick them up and get going! Rely on the resources God has already given you.

1. Your dreams. You might say "Dreams! Is that all? What are dreams good for? What can I do with dreams?" My friend, every great accomplishment began as a dream. The first automobile, airplane, and space shuttle all started in the human imagination. Neil Armstrong's footsteps on the moon were the fulfillment of decades of dreams—the dreams of science fiction writers and engineers and an American president, John

THE POWER OF ONE

F. Kennedy, who was assassinated before he could see the dream come true.

America was a dream in the minds of the Pilgrims, the Jamestown colonists, the revolutionaries, and the Founding Fathers. Millions of Americans of all races have freedom, equality, and opportunities that their parents and grandparents never dreamed of—and why? Because Dr. Martin Luther King, Jr. had a dream, and he dared to make that dream come true.

Shamgar dreamed of liberating his people from the terrorism and oppression of the Philistines. Then he took up his ox goad and made that dream a reality. So, what are your dreams? Have you taken the time to look beyond what is and envision what could be?

Dreams are compelling. They fill us with hope. They enable us to imagine a better tomorrow. They motivate us and energize us. They activate our courage so that we will dare to take risks to see our dreams come true. Our dreams should be bold, audacious, and even a bit scary. Johann Wolfgang von Goethe wrote: "Dream no small dreams for they have no power to move the hearts of men."

Dream big dreams, then dare to do whatever it takes to hammer those dreams into reality. The former center of the Orlando Magic, Zaza Pachulia, was born in Tbilisi, Georgia, in the former Soviet Union. His mother, Marina, was a big basketball fan, and Zaza caught basketball fever from his mom when he was nine years old. He papered the walls of his bedroom with pictures of Michael Jordan. Marina would use basketball to motivate Zaza to work and study hard. If his school grades slipped, she would hide his basketball and shoes until his grades improved. At night, Marina would tuck Zaza into bed and tell him a bedtime story: "Once upon a time, there was a boy who grew up to play basketball in the NBA. The crowds cheered him in every big city across the U.S.A., because he made every shot, and he scooped up every rebound." Every day and every night, Zaza dreamed of playing basketball. Zaza Pachulia lived his hardwood dreams as a former NBA player for the Magic, the Bucks, the Hawks, the Mavericks, the Warriors, and now the basketball operations consultant for the Golden State Warriors. I heard him say one evening, "All I ever dreamed about is the NBA and now I am here."

Dreams are a powerful, life changing resource. Don't ever say you have no resources to accomplish great things. Everyone has the power to dream, and dreaming is the first step to achieving. The bigger your dream, the greater your accomplishment. People will tell you, "Don't be such a dreamer! Be practical!" Half of the people who tell you that mean well—they don't want you to be disappointed when you fall short of your dreams. The other half are envious of your dreams; they're afraid you'll succeed, and they won't. Whether they mean well or not, those who try to squash your dreams are not doing you any favors. Don't listen to them. Just keep on dreaming.

Let me tell you something about you that you may not even be aware of, but it's true: you were born for greatness! I mean that with all my heart. You may say, "But Pat, you don't even know me! How can you say I was born for greatness?" Answer: because we were all born for greatness. We were all created in the image and likeness of God, and God designed us to do great things.

I'm not saying you were necessarily born to be rich or famous or to alter the fate of nations. But true greatness rarely has anything to do with such things. The truly great people in this world are the ones who dream of making a difference in lives, even if it's only a few lives. Great people will take the time to make a difference in the lives of needy children, or people in a retirement home, or veterans in a VA hospital, or people who are trapped in poverty or addiction, or shut up behind prison walls.

Anyone can be great because anyone can reach out and make a difference in the lives of other people. Dream great dreams, just as God intended you to. Then make those dreams come true and become the person God made you to be. Shamgar had a dream and an ox goad, and he saved his people. What is your big dream?

2. Your Enthusiasm – John Marcus Templeton once defined enthusiasm as "that state of exuberance in which all things seem possible." Even overcoming 600-

to-one odds? I don't believe Shamgar could have done what he did without enthusiasm, without that wild-eyed belief that, through the power of God, all things were possible.

Enthusiasm is energy. It electrifies the soul. Plug into the power of enthusiasm and you'll be amazed at what you will accomplish. The poet Ralph Waldo Emerson once put it this way: "Every great and commanding movement in the annals of the world is a triumph of enthusiasm."

You might say, "But I don't have any enthusiasm." To which I would reply, "Why not? If you believe in God, you should be overflowing with enthusiasm!" After all, the word enthusiasm comes from the Greek word *entheos,* which means, "in God." If you are "in God" and if God is in you, then your life should be brimming with enthusiasm, energy, and inspiration.

Beethoven always believed that when he was composing music, he was in tune with his Creator. On one occasion, he introduced one of his newly written symphonies to an orchestra. In the middle of the rehearsal, one of the violinists stood up and complained, "This section is so difficult and awkward that it is simply unplayable! Beethoven glared at the violinist. "When I composed that passage," he said, "I was inspired by Almighty God, the Maker of the universe! Do you think I can consider your puny little fiddle when God speaks through me."

THE POWER OF ONE

That's enthusiasm talking! That is a man filled with *entheos!* As someone once said, "Enthusiasm is faith set on fire." If you truly have faith in God, you can't help having enthusiasm. If you truly have something to be enthusiastic about, then you have a reason for living. Former Milwaukee Bucks all-star forward Marques Johnson put it this way: "It's the sport that I love, not the business. The business end messes everything up. I almost wish there was no money in it. Then we could all go out and enjoy playing like we did when we were kids. I'd still play if there was no money, because it's the best game there is, and you can play all the time if you want. Anybody who's ever been into it, pro or playground, knows what I'm talking about. When I'm playing ball, it's like I'm not even part of the Earth. It's like I belong to a different universe." That's enthusiasm! That's *entheos!*

Enthusiasm makes your mind sharper, your arm stronger, and your feet swifter. Enthusiasm lifts your spirits and fires up your will to persevere. Enthusiasm motivates and empowers you. Enthusiasm can often compensate for a lack of money, skill, or talent. A plan that might otherwise fail often succeeds on the strength of enthusiasm alone.

If you lack enthusiasm, then pray for it. Ask God to fill up your soul with a passionate enthusiasm to do his will and to accomplish the great life's mission he has given you. The Bible is filled with enthusiastic expressions of praise to God and confidence in his ability to do anything through us, even the seemingly "impossible." Here are just a few examples:

Shout for joy to God, all the earth! Sing the glory of his name; make his praise glorious. Psalm 66:1

My lips will shout for joy when I sing praise to you— I whom you have delivered. Psalm 71:23

"Everything is possible for one who believes" Mark 9:23b

I can do all this through Him who gives me strength. Phil 4:13

That is the enthusiasm and confidence that comes with authentic faith in God. If we believe in God, it should show on our faces, it should turbocharge our voices, it should fill us with a confidence that everything is possible because we are possessed by *entheos*. God is in us! Writer Maurice Boyd tells of the time conductor Eugene Ormandy dislocated his shoulder while conducting a symphony by Brahms. In the margin of the score, Brahms had written at one point, "As loud as possible!" Then, a few measures later, he wrote, "Louder still!" It was at that point that Ormandy conducted so vigorously, athletically, and enthusiastically that he threw his shoulder out of joint.

Boyd concluded, "and have never had an enthusiasm great enough to dislodge a necktie, let alone their shoulder."

THE POWER OF ONE

What about you? What is the one thing in life that fills you with a joint-straining, body-spraining enthusiasm? Writer Diane Ackerman once expressed a conviction that should be your life's goal and mine." I don't want to get to the end of my life and find that I lived just the length of it. I want to have lived the width of it as well."

Andy Russell was a legendary Steelers linebacker — a gap-toothed, roaring leader dubbed as Pittsburgh's "Steel Curtain Defense." Russell once recalled how he learned the true depth of enthusiasm from defensive tackle Ernie Stautner.

Ernie comes into the huddle and his thumb is broken back against his wrist. There's a tear near the break and his bone's sticking out. He has a compound fracture of the thumb. He takes his thumb in his hand, and he wrenches it down into his fist. Doesn't show it to anybody. Doesn't say anything. Looks up and says, "What's the defense?" I thought to myself, "I'm not in the right business!"

So, he stayed there for the rest of that series and then we came off the field. I'm watching him because I'm the only guy who saw that he had a compound fracture. I saw the bone. So, I'm figuring now he's going to ask for a doctor, and he may have to go to the hospital, because this thing could get infected.

But he says, "Give me some tape." So, they throw him some tape, and he just starts taping this huge ball.

He makes this big fist; then, we go back in. He plays the entire game, never misses a down. I'm just astounded and he's using this hand, which is broken, as a club. He's beating people with it.

After the game, we go into the locker room and he says, "Hey, Doc, I think I got a problem," and I'm thinking, "This is just unbelievable!" That is passion for what you do. That guy was making no money. He just loved to play.

That's the power of enthusiasm. It can make you indomitable, undefeatable, even when your body is broken and wracked with pain. Enthusiasm can lift you above adversity and give you the winning edge.

3. Your Talent - "If we did all the things we are capable of doing, we would astonish ourselves." So said the astonishing Thomas Alva Edison, the Wizard of Menlo Park, the inventor of nearly 1,400 patented inventions. It's true. We are capable of so much more than we dream or imagine. If we would simply start using even 10 percent of the talent and ability we have, we would probably be amazed at how much we could accomplish. It has been said that it was amateurs who built Noah's Ark, but professionals built the Titanic. Great achievements are often produced by people of relatively modest talent who are willing to offer it all to God for the service of others. Shamgar was a farmer, not a warrior, yet he offered whatever talents he had to God, and God used him to save a nation.

THE POWER OF ONE

Don Shula, the winningest coach in NFL history, once said this about players with talent: "Coaches tend to stay too long with people with 'potential.' Try to avoid those players and go with a proven attitude. Players who live on 'potential' are coach-killers. As soon as you find out who the coach-killers are on your team, the better off you are. Go with the guys who have less talent, but more dedication, more singleness of purpose."

If you tell me, "I can't accomplish anything, I don't have any talent," I want you to know that you have all the talent you need. The only thing you lack is a willingness to use the talents you have! You may not have the entrepreneurial ability of Bill Gates, the writing ability of James Michener, the artistic ability of Picasso, the athletic ability of Michael Jordan or the preaching ability of Billy Graham, but so what? You have all the ability you need to carry out the mission God has given you—if you will put 100 percent of your ability to use for God.

Billy Sunday, the great preacher of the early twentieth century, said, "More people fail through lack of purpose more than through lack of talent." What most of us need is not more talent, but the willingness to do more with the talent we have. Don't worry about being the best. Just make the best of the talents you have.

Composer Igor Stravinsky was once approached by a film producer to write a movie score. Stravinsky listened as the producer described the script and told him who would star in the film—but when the producer mentioned the fee, Stravinsky jumped to his feet. "Four thousand dollars!" he said. "You expect me to score an entire film for four thousand dollars!" The producer told Stravinsky that another famous composer had recently completed a picture for the very same amount. "But there's no comparison!" Stravinsky countered. "He's a much more talented composer than I am! I have very little talent, so for me the work is much more difficult and will take me much longer to complete. I could not accept the assignment for anything less than eight thousand dollars." The producer met Stravinsky's price.

You may think you have very little talent—but you have enough talent for any challenge you face. Your responsibility is to make the most of the talent you have. It was given to you for a reason. Find it. Use it.

4. Your Education: Melville Weston Fuller was Chief Justice of the U.S. Supreme Court over a century ago. He was also very much involved in his church. Once, while he chaired a church conference, one of the conference speakers got up and spoke for half an hour on the evil influence of higher education. The man actually gave thanks to God that his mind had never been "polluted" by the wicked teachings of a university. Fuller listened to this man until he could stand no more. He rose to his feet and interrupted the speaker. "Am I to understand, sir," Fuller said, "that you are giving thanks to God for the blessings of ignorance? The man looked a little confused, then replied, "Well, yes, I suppose I am" "In that case," Fuller said, "you have much to be thankful for."

I don't know how much education Shamgar had. He probably had little formal schooling—but he clearly had enough education to complete the mission God gave him. His education may have consisted of hearing the stories of Israel's heroes—Abraham, Isaac, Jacob, Joseph, Moses, and Joshua. Perhaps he learned military tactics by sitting around a campfire and listening to his father, Anath, recount the stories of Joshua's battles at Hazor and Jericho. Perhaps he learned stealth and guerilla tactics from the account of Joshua and Caleb's spy mission in the land of Canaan.

What kind of education do you have? An MBA or a PhD? A bachelor's degree in arts or science? A high school diploma? Or a head full of street smarts from the School of Hard Knocks? Whatever your level of education, that is a resource you can use to achieve your life goals and to fulfill your God-given mission in life.

Albert Einstein, who gave us the theory of relativity, once said, "Education is that which remains when you have forgotten everything you learned in school." That's so true! Most of us think that education is something you pour into an empty skull during four or more years at a university. In reality, the purpose of a university is not to *complete* the process of education but to ignite a lifelong love affair with learning.

As the late billionaire publisher Malcolm Forbes said, "The purpose of education is to replace an empty mind with an open mind." In other words, to be educated does not merely mean that you have learned what you need to know. It means that you know how to learn, how to unlearn, and how to relearn. The world is changing too quickly to allow your knowledge level to remain static. Changes in society, the economy and technology are taking place so rapidly that what was true this morning may no longer be true this afternoon.

According to Hamilton Securities of Washington, D.C., if we represented the population of the entire world as a village of 100 people, it would look like this: There would be 14 North and South Americans, 21 Europeans, 8 Africans and 57 Asians. Fully 70 of those 100 people would be nonwhite and an equal number would be non-Christian. Half of the world's wealth would be in the hands of 6 people. No fewer than 80 of those 100 people would live in substandard housing, 70 would be illiterate and 50 would suffer from malnutrition. And here's one final statistic that should change the way you look at your life: *Only one of those 100 people would have a college education.*

What about you? Do you have a college education? If you do, you have a resource in your hand that 99 percent of the people in this world do not have. What are you doing with that resource? That diploma of yours is your ox goad. Use that educated mind of yours.

THE POWER OF ONE

5. Your Experience. Dr. John MacArthur is the pastor of Grace Community Church in Sun Valley, California. As a 21-year-old college football player, he was honored with a trophy at an awards banquet. He got up to speak and in the course of his short acceptance speech, he talked about his love for Jesus Christ. After the banquet, a man came to him and said, "There is a girl in the hospital who really needs your help. She's really depressed and needs to hear what you said tonight about Jesus Christ. I'm not a pastor or a counselor," MacArthur said. "You don't have to be," the man said. "Just tell her what you told everyone tonight. You don't have to preach. Just tell her your story."

MacArthur went to the hospital. The girl in the hospital bed was an attractive high school cheerleader named Polly. She was depressed because her boyfriend accidentally shot her in the neck, severing her spinal cord. Polly was paralyzed for life. Young John MacArthur haltingly introduced himself, then said, "I can't imagine what you are going through. "If I had a way to do it, I'd kill myself," Polly replied bitterly. "I don't have any reason to live." MacArthur didn't know what else to say, so he started telling the same story he had told at the awards banquet—the story of how he had given his life to Jesus Christ. He wasn't sure if Polly was even listening, but he kept talking.

Finally, he said, "You know, it's not what happens to your body that matters. It's what happens to your eternal soul. I know it's hard for you to understand this now, but I'm sure that God can bring joy into your heart, even after all that you are going through. But first you have to decide where you will spend eternity. Would you like to hear how you can know that you will spend eternity in heaven with Christ?" "Sure," she said. "Tell me. I'm desperate." The young football player told Polly that Jesus had nailed her sins to the cross so that she could be forgiven and cleansed. When he had finished, he said, "Polly, would you like to commit your life to Jesus Christ and receive him as your Lord and Savior?"

"Yes," she whispered. "I would," and they prayed together.

For months afterward, John would return to the hospital and visit Polly. She had up days and down days, but she was clearly changed. The bitterness and suicidal depression were things of the past. On one visit, she said, "In some ways, John, I'm glad this happened to me. If it hadn't, I wouldn't know Jesus."

John MacArthur kept in touch with Polly, and in time, she met and married a Christian man who loved her regardless of her disability. But not only was Polly's life changed by this experience—so was MacArthur's. The experience of being used by God in this way completely changed the way he viewed his own life. He said to himself, "Running around on a field with a football under my arm means nothing. Touching lives with the love of Jesus Christ—that's what matters. Reaching others with the power of the Gospel is all I want for my life. Nothing else even comes close."

This experience was the turning point that led John MacArthur into ministry. That hospital visit led to 64 years and counting of McArthur pastoring the Grace Community Church. He has written more commentaries, books, and edited study Bibles than fit on one page.

What are the experiences that God wants to use in your life? No matter what other resources we think we lack, we can't deny that we have experience. Every day we spend on this planet is one more day of experience. Our experiences may not all be triumphs and successes, but so what? Failure is usually a far better teacher than success—if we are willing to learn the lessons. As former Houston Astros pitcher and manager Larry Dierker observed, "Experience is the best teacher, but a hard grader. She gives the test first, the lesson later."

Isn't *that* the truth! Sometimes it seems that experience is a thing that we don't get until after we need it! But if we approach our lives with a positive and teachable attitude, we will learn the lessons of our experiences in time for the next big test. We should always remember that experience is not what happens in our lives, but *how we respond* to what happens in our lives. The poet Archibald McLeish once said, "There is only one thing more painful than learning from experience and that is *not* learning from experience." A great deal depends on our attitude toward our mistakes:

It is much more helpful and useful to think of them as "experiences" rather than "failures." The word "failure" suggests "The End," but the word "experience" conveys the idea of a detour on the road to success.

I have given a lot of thought to how Shamgar could have gained the military experience to single-handedly destroy a force of 600 Philistine warriors, armed only with an ox goad. The answer kept coming back to me: he couldn't have had any military experience. Not only did Israel have no king and no army, but the nation had not had a war in eighty years. I asked myself: What kind of experience did he have? Answer: He must have been an experienced *hunter*.

Think about it: The oxen on his farm were for pulling a plow, not for making ox burgers or oxtail soup. He probably raised wheat on his farm, which was a staple in the diet of Middle Eastern people 3,000 years ago. What, then, did Shamgar do for meat? Most likely, he hunted. What did he hunt with? He had no bow and arrow, or he would have used such a weapon against the Philistines. He must have hunted with his ox goad, using it as a club or a spear. When the Philistines invaded Israel, what did he do? He did what he had always done. He did what his experience had taught him to do.

He hunted. He picked up his ox goad and used it the same way he had used it to hunt bears, mountain lions, and deer. Only this time he hunted Philistines. He started where he was, he used what he had—his ox goad and his experience as a hunter—and he did what he could. That is a powerful lesson for your life and mine.

With every experience in life, whether good or bad, pleasant, or painful, we should ask ourselves, "How can I put that experience to good use? What can I learn from that? What is the lesson I can apply to my life my career, my ministry, my relationships? "All the things that happen to us—a breakdown on the freeway, getting fired from a job, serving on a jury, going through bankruptcy—are experiences that can increase our character and wisdom. But we only grow from them if we actively, prayerfully look for the lessons that are embedded in those experiences. The French philosopher and novelist Albert Camus wisely said, "You cannot create experience. You must undergo it." In other words, we cannot manufacture our experiences. We cannot always choose what we will experience. Life comes to us whether we are ready or not. Our job is to undergo our experiences, accept them, learn from them, and recognize that everything we go through is part of God's grand plan to mold us and shape our character.

6. Your Influence David Blankenhorn, founder of the Institute for American Values and author of Fatherless America tells the story of a man who entered a barbershop and began talking to a teenage boy who was sweeping the floor. As they talked, the man realized that the boy had no father. As they talked, the man realized that the boy had no father. "Son," he asked, "who would you want to be like when you grow up?" "Mister," the boy said with an edge of bitterness in his voice,

"I ain't never met nobody I want to be like when I grow up." Those words break my heart.

Young people need heroes and role models. They need people who will *influence* them to become all that they are capable of becoming. We all have the gift of influence. We influence others through our words, our example, our caring, and our actions. We can't help but influence others. The only choice we have is whether our influence is for good or ill.

People are watching us all the time, even when we don't realize it. They notice when our talk and our walk don't match. They can spot hypocrisy in an instant. If you want to be a person of influence, then be a hero and a role model to the people around you.

Actress and country music star Reba McEntire once put it this way: "Our kids need heroes. Our kids need somebody to look up to, and y'all are it." She's right. Look at the children and teenagers around you, in your home, your neighborhood, your church. They are looking for people of character and integrity, people to pattern their lives after. They need heroes—and y'all are it.

My life has been shaped by my heroes and mentors. One of those heroes was Andy Seminick—the famed Phillies catcher of the late 1940s and early '50s. When I was a boy, Andy was my idol. Fact is, he's one of the reasons I wanted to be a catcher when I got into college and professional baseball.

I had gotten to know Andy while I was a teenager, hanging around Shibe Park in Philadelphia. He was one of the Whiz Kids, the National League pennant-winning Phillies of 1950. In 1962, when I started playing pro baseball with the Miami Marlins of the Florida State League, the manager of the club was none other than Andy Seminick, my boyhood hero.

I spent two years playing for Andy, and he had an enormous influence on my life. One of the values Andy drilled into us was tenacity: "You've got to be tough," he often said, "and you've got to play hurt." You want to know what kind of influence Andy Seminick had on me? I'll tell you.

In January 1997, thirty-five years after I had first played for Andy, I played in a Phillies/Cardinals Dream Week game in St. Petersburg, Florida—what they call "an old-timers' game." I was behind the plate, catching at age fifty-six. Larry Andersen, the former major league reliever, was pitching.

Larry threw a hard slider, and I caught it right on the thumb of my catching hand. I felt a bolt of electric pain, and I saw that the top joint of my left thumb was completely knocked out of the socket. I ran over to the dugout and called for the trainer, who pulled on the joint and popped it back into place. That thumb was still throbbing—but I ran back to the plate and continued catching. Why did I keep playing? Because Andy Seminick, my boyhood idol and first pro manager, was on the bench in the dugout. Even though he was seventy-six years old by that time, and I was fifty-six, I could still hear his voice in my brain, saying, "You've got to be tough, and you've got to play hurt. So, I went back in the game and played hurt for Andy." Now, *that* is influence!

My greatest hero is Jesus of Nazareth, a man who had more lasting influence on the world than any other human being in history. He spent three intense years pouring his life into twelve men. Though he preached to the masses, he concentrated his influence in the lives of a few individuals. He deeply and profoundly influenced twelve men, and through them, he changed the world.

Jesus practiced his influence on others by being an example and a role model. When he wanted to teach his disciples about prayer, he didn't say, "You ought to get on your knees and say these words." He took them out into the olive grove and prayed with them all night long. When he wanted to teach them what it means to serve others, he didn't say, "Here's what you need to do." He got down on his knees, took a basin and towel, washed their feet, and set an example for them to follow. That's influence. Jesus didn't just say, "Listen to me." He said, "Follow me. Learn from my example. Do as I do." If we want to have an influence on the people around us, then we need to become heroes and role models. We need to

THE POWER OF ONE

get down in the trenches with people and pour our lives into their lives.

When I think of Shamgar, I wonder what kind of influence he had with his friends and neighbors. He was probably respected as a local businessman, a farmer, a man who grew the grain that helped feed his community. But I suspect that when he went to his neighbors with a plan to drive the Philistines out of their land, his influence reached its limit. I can picture Shamgar calling his neighbors together to discuss the Philistine problem. I can imagine him telling his friends, "We have to band together and drive these Philistines out of our land! If we work together, we can defeat them! Now, every man who's with me, step forward!"

And I can see all of Shamgar's trembling neighbors taking three steps back! "Look, Shamgar," one of them might have said, "You're a fine wheat farmer and a real asset to our community. But let's face it—you're no Joshua! There isn't one true military genius in all of Israel. We all just want to hold on and keep our families hidden until the Philistines get tired of killing us and decide to go home. If you want to attack them, go ahead—but you'll have to attack them alone."

So Shamgar did exactly that! After single-handedly expanded enormously! From then on, Shamgar was recognized as a judge over all of Israel— and a person of national influence.

Our influence must be used responsibly. Hall of Fame baseball manager Sparky Anderson put it bluntly: *Athletes who say they ain't role models for our youth...don't deserve a dime of their millions. They're totally missing the boat. God gave them all this special ability, and then they take the money and snub their noses at the kids or anybody who happens to be in their way. They've got to understand that they have the chance to be a leader. They can teach our young people by the way they live their lives.*

Whether they like it or not, every athlete is a role model. So is every adult. Our children look up to us. Every day, we get the chance to influence more young lives than we can ever imagine. Sometimes, it just takes a smile or a pat on the shoulder. Maybe all it takes is a couple of minutes to listen to a youngster's problems. I believe that if an athlete does something dumb, like getting hooked on drugs or alcohol, he should then be penalized double. That's the price for abusing the precious gift they've been given.

To be a person of influence, you don't have to be a basketball star. You don't have to be a person of great status and station in life. No matter who you are and what you do, you are a person of influence. You have the opportunity to impact the lives of many people every day—family, friends, neighbors, coworkers, young people, old people and even the people you meet along life's way. What kind of influence are you having on the lives around you? How are you using the God-given resource of your influence on others?

7. Your Wisdom. Another resource that most of us have (but are quick to overlook) is our wisdom. I'm not talking about intelligence, knowledge, or education. There are many people who are not particularly well educated but are amazingly wise. And there are also people who could achieve a perfect score on the Mensa test, yet who are utterly bankrupt in the wisdom department. As someone once said, "Never mistake knowledge for wisdom. One helps you make a living; the other helps you make a life."

When I was young, I was very impressed by people who were smart or talented or gifted in some way. As I've grown older, I've become much more impressed by people who are wise, who have a deep understanding of life, those who can explain how to live effectively for God and for others. Where does wisdom come from? The Bible tells us, *"If any of you lacks wisdom, you should ask God, who gives generously to all without finding fault, and it will be given to you."* (James 1:5).

Former National Security Advisor Condoleezza Rice is a devout Christian and a woman of prayer. Once, when she was asked what she prays for, she said, "I was taught that you don't pray with a laundry list. So, I ask for wisdom and guidance and strength of conviction."

We gain wisdom as we cooperate with God while he seeks to shape and mold our lives. Wisdom doesn't come to us all at once like a bolt of lightning. It is built up gradually within us as we learn and grow from the many experiences that life sends our way. We become wiser as we become more patient, tolerant, caring, compassionate, loving, understanding and insightful. We become wiser as we learn to trust God more completely through the tests and trials of life.

The most important use of wisdom is in making good decisions. As Bible teacher Charles Swindoll once said, "Since wisdom is God's specialty, it's imperative that we seek his wisdom prior to every major decision." The wiser we become, the more we are able to see life from God's perspective—and the easier it becomes to make good decisions in difficult circumstances.

No question, as Shamgar faced the great crisis of his life—the invasion of his homeland by the Philistines—he needed more than his trusty ox goad at his side. He needed wisdom. He needed help from God in making a tough decision: Should he go out alone, braving impossible odds, to fight the enemy? Or should he pack up his family and his belongings and seek safety until the Philistines had left? I have no doubt that Shamgar spent long hours on his knees before God, seeking divine wisdom for a painfully difficult decision. In the end, wisdom told Shamgar to stay and fight. He had no guarantee that he would win. But he had to start where he was, use what he had, and do what he could.

THE POWER OF ONE

He mustered up his courage, his skill, and his wisdom—then with ox goad in hand, he fought.

Another Shamgar-minded man was Dietrich Bonhoeffer. He was a pastor and theologian in the German Lutheran church in the 1930s. He watched with horror and disgust as the Nazi Party took over his nation—and as his fellow German churchmen began siding with the Nazis. In 1933, even before Hitler came to power, Bonhoeffer spoke out in a series of radio broadcasts in which he called for the German people to reject the Nazis and defend the rights of the Jewish minority. By 1935, Bonhoeffer had become a leader in the Confessing Church, a wing of the Lutheran church that remained faithful to the gospel of Christian love and peace and that struggled against the increasing Nazification of German Christianity. He established an underground seminary that taught not only the Bible and theology, but the principles of nonviolent resistance. In 1937, the Nazi secret police (the Gestapo) closed the seminary and jailed many of the ministers of the Confessing Church. In 1939, American theologian Reinhold Niebuhr helped secure a position for Bonhoeffer at Union Theological Seminary in New York. But after only three weeks in the United States, Bonhoeffer decided to return to Germany to suffer with his people. "I have had time to think and to pray about my situation," he said in a public statement. "I have come to the conclusion that I have made a mistake in coming to America. I shall have no right to participate in the reconstruction of the Christian life in Germany after the war if I did not share in the trials of this time with my people."

In 1941, Bonhoeffer joined Operation 7, an underground resistance and rescue movement that helped Jews escape to safety in Switzerland. By 1942, his involvement in the resistance took a fateful turn: Bonhoeffer joined a plot to assassinate Hitler.

The decision to take part in the death of another human being was a difficult one for Dietrich Bonhoeffer. He spent uncounted hours on his knees, imploring God for wisdom. Bonhoeffer was a pastor, a man of the Gospel, a committed pacifist. He had always taught his seminary students to seek a nonviolent solution to injustice. Murder was always wrong, he believed.

Yet he knew that the German state was committing mass murder on a scale unprecedented in human history. The fanatical hatred of one man, Adolf Hitler, was slaughtering millions of human beings. If he could help end the Nazi genocide by the assassination of Adolf Hitler, would it truly be murder? Or would it be an act of holy obedience, mercy, and love? Though he prayed and prayed, Bonhoeffer could not decide whether killing Hitler would be right or wrong.

Despite his moral uncertainty, Bonhoeffer came to a practical, logical decision that it had to be done. As he told his sister-in-law, Emmi Bonhoeffer, "If I see a madman driving a car into a group of innocent bystanders, then I can't as a Christian simply wait for the catastrophe, then comfort the wounded and bury the dead. I must try to wrestle the steering wheel out of the hands of the driver."

Bonhoeffer joined the conspiracy — a secret group that operated inside German Military Intelligence. Bonhoeffer's fellow conspirators included Admiral Wilhelm Canaris (head of Military Intelligence), General Hans Oster and Hans von Dohnanyi (the husband of Bonhoeffer's sister, Christine). Bonhoeffer acted as a courier, carrying messages to the Allies on behalf of the resistance. During his involvement in the plot against Hitler, Bonhoeffer was living in a Benedictine monastery near Munich, working on a book entitled Ethics. As you read that book, you discover that he was actually searching his mind and soul for wisdom for making difficult moral decisions in a time of extreme crisis. Even while he was taking part in an attempted coupd'état, he was writing a book and seeking answers to the moral and spiritual questions that troubled his soul.

In April 1943, Bonhoeffer and several of his associates were arrested by the Gestapo for their involvement with Operation 7—but the Gestapo agents didn't know about his involvement in the plot against Hitler. The thirty-seven-year-old Bonhoeffer was taken to Tegel Prison in Berlin; also arrested were his brother-in-law and sister, Hans and Christine von Dohnanyi.

Bonhoeffer spent the next two years in prison. Meanwhile, several assassination attempts were aborted. Finally, on July 20, 1944, Colonel Claus von Stauffenberg carried a briefcase bomb into a conference attended by Hitler. The colonel placed the briefcase under the table next to Hitler, then left the room, supposedly to make a phone call. The bomb exploded, killing four of Hitler's top officers. Hitler himself, however, had gotten up from the table moments before the bomb exploded. He survived the blast with a badly injured right arm.

Admiral Canaris was arrested, along with others who had conspired against Hitler—but the Gestapo still knew nothing of Bonhoeffer's involvement in the plot. In February 1945, Bonhoeffer was moved to the Buchenwald concentration camp. Two months later, the Nazis discovered Bonhoeffer's name in the diary of Admiral Canaris. An enraged Adolf Hitler personally demanded the execution of Canaris, Bonhoeffer, the Dohnanyi and anyone else involved in the assassination attempt. In April 1945, Bonhoeffer was moved to the prison at Flossenburg, where Canaris was also held. His execution was set for the morning of April 9. That morning, the prison doctor found Dietrich Bonhoeffer kneeling before God, praying with such intensity that he wasn't even aware of the doctor's presence.

A short time later, Bonhoeffer was led from his cell to a scaffold in the prison courtyard. He went calmly and quietly. On the scaffold, he again knelt to pray one last time. Then the rope was placed around his neck, the floor dropped from beneath his feet, and Dietrich Bonhoeffer went into the presence of his God. The tragic irony of Bonhoeffer's death is that, less than three weeks after he was hanged, Hitler committed suicide in a Berlin bunker. Germany surrendered a week after Hitler's death. So, in one sense, it seems that Bonhoeffer died for nothing. The plot failed, and Hitler eventually died anyway. If Bonhoeffer had simply stayed out of the plot against Hitler, he could have lived. Instead, he died at the age of thirty-nine.

But not so fast - Bonhoeffer did what he had to do, just as Shamgar did. Neither Bonhoeffer nor Shamgar had any assurance that their missions would end in victory. Happily, Shamgar defeated the Philistines. Bonhoeffer's mission failed, and he lost his life. Even so, both Bonhoeffer and Shamgar did the right thing. Acting in God's wisdom, they opposed evil. Each, in his own way, sought to preserve his people and save his nation. Here, then, are two great examples for us to follow. There is no guarantee that our plans will succeed. But success is not the important thing. The results are ultimately God's responsibility—and God measures success differently than we do. Our job is to simply start where we are, use what we have, and do what we can, and very often those courageous actions will empower another to do the same. Those are the legacies we will not know until heaven.

So, my friend, it's time to take stock of your God-given resources. Ask yourself, "What do I have to complete my mission in life? What is my ox goad?" Once you have your ox goad in hand, then leap into action!

FIVE

The Practice of Creativity

– Jay Strack

"Creativity is seeing what others see and thinking what no one else ever thought." – Albert Einstein

As I teach at SLU, "A goal is a dream with details, direction, and a deadline." Imagination and creativity are the playgrounds of your dreams where ideas skip about in our heads until one sticks and fascinates us. Then, we proceed to write down small steps and formulate a plan. The habit of thinking deeply without distraction creates opportunities to free-float ideas, imagine designs and inventions, consider the impossible, and solve problems.

Biographies are my favorite genre of books to read because I get fresh ideas and learn dos and don'ts. Whether I study clergy, executives, sports figures, politicians, or everyday moms and dads, I am fascinated by those who go against the odds and how they do it. I may not agree with the person's worldview, but I can still gather valuable take-a-ways. With each bio, I take the time to imagine how I would have handled the situation. These "lessons" I write down and keep in notebooks piled in my study. For me, writing thoughts down makes them more accessible in my mind. Philosopher Jean-Jacques Rousseau wrote, "The world of reality has its limits; the world of imagination is boundless." Although I have had the privilege of visiting more than 30 nations, I travel to the land of "Imagination" most often.

That may be why I am a longtime NASA enthusiast. On the wall behind my desk is a collection of NASA badges, astronauts' autographs, and quotes, the most prominently displayed being the words of Gene Kranz, "Failure is not an option." The life of Kranz fascinates me. Two other Kranz quotes are circled in my copy of his autobiography: "To recognize that the greatest error is not to have tried and failed, but that in trying, we did not give it our best effort," and "There is no such thing as good enough. You, your team, and your equipment must be the best. That is how you will win victories."

Kranz was the flight director of Apollo 13, the infamous mission that gave us the all-purpose quote, "Houston, we have a problem." During the first two days of the Apollo 13 lunar mission, the space engineers at NASA Mission Control called it the smoothest flight in the history of the space program. The mission scoffed at the superstition associated with the number 13, choosing to schedule the landing of the 13th space exploration for April 13th, 1970.

THE POWER OF ONE

All was calm, at first. Near the end of the mission's second day, the CAPCOM (capsule communicator) in Houston radioed the spacecraft, "We're bored to tears down here." About nine hours after that comment, all boredom abruptly ended. That was when Mission Control directed astronaut Jack Swigert to stir the cryogenic tanks—the spherical tanks that contained a slush of super-cold oxygen. Unfortunately, no one knew that the tanks had been damaged and that they had been fitted with the wrong thermostatic switches.

Soon after Swigert began stirring the tanks, the spacecraft's hull rang like a church bell struck by a two-ton hammer. The spacecraft's number two oxygen tank exploded, causing a reactionary failure in the number one tank. Two of the ship's three fuel cells were also disabled, resulting in a severe power loss. The vessel and its three-man crew were 200,000 miles from home, rapidly losing power, light, oxygen, and water.

Swigert reported to Mission Control: "Houston, we have a problem." At first, the three astronauts were only concerned with one question: Can we still go to the moon? Within minutes, however, it became clear that they faced a bigger question: Will we ever make it home?

The crew only had one option: shut down all systems to conserve power, scramble into Aquarius's lunar module, and use it as a lifeboat. Aquarius was equipped to sustain two men for two days during a lunar landing and return. For the crew to survive, it would have to support three men for four days. Neither the three astronauts in orbit nor the engineers in Houston knew how to make it happen, but they knew Aquarius was the only hope.

Going back in time was not an option. The crew had to start where they were, use what they had, and do what they could. NASA engineers began by listing the problems that had to be solved and then brainstorming all possible solutions. The first problem was the rising level of poisonous carbon dioxide and the low oxygen reserves. The filters aboard Aquarius were not designed to handle the carbon dioxide output of three astronauts.

The engineers in Houston came up with a plan. Someone brought a box and said, "fill it with every piece of trash, paper, equipment, clothing, or resource" that could be found in the capsule. Pouring the entire box onto a table, they scrambled ideas and experimented with makeshift scenarios. They finally devised a plan for carbon dioxide filters constructed from plastic bags, cardboard, and tape and sent the plan to space. The astronauts completed the construction of the filters just as the carbon dioxide in the spacecraft was reaching a critical level.

Meanwhile, power consumption was cut to the bone. Engineers in Houston carefully computed how much power was needed to get home versus how much power remained in the batteries. There was scarcely a single ampere-hour of juice to spare.

THE POWER OF ONE

Water consumption was also severely restricted since it was used for drinking and cooling critical mechanical systems. Each crewman was allowed six ounces of water daily, a fifth of the usual intake. Before the end of the flight, all three men were severely dehydrated and had lost a total of 31.5 pounds during their flight.

Because the spacecraft was headed for the moon at the time of the explosion, it was in no position for a return-to-earth trajectory. A new course had to be computed for Apollo 13, which would swing the craft around the moon and back toward Earth for the return trip home. Ordinarily, the course would be aligned by a device called the "alignment optical telescope," which would locate a navigational star. The spacecraft, however, was surrounded by a cloud of debris from the explosion, making the alignment telescope useless. Once again, the astronauts had to use what they had to do what they could. Since they lacked a distant star to steer by, they devised a plan to use the sun itself as a navigational star.[17]

Talk about creativity! Team thinking and innovation were essential. No idea was too small or too crazy to be considered. With intense teamwork, the crew of *Apollo 13* managed to reenter the earth's atmosphere at just the right angle. The crippled spacecraft splashed down in the South Pacific where the helicopter carrier

U.S.S. *Iwo Jima* retrieved the crew. The creativity and cumulative thinking made the impossible possible.

You may think, "That's a great story, but I won't ever be in that situation." Probably not, but you will have to navigate life's challenges. Everything from difficult people to lack of resources to diminished health and beyond. You choose in those moments to pull a team together, re-think resources, and make it happen, or to give in to despair.

Think Creatively!

If you want to have the brave heartbeat of Shamgar, you must embrace the time-worn phrase, "think outside the box."

An outside-the-box thinker can turn plastic bags, cardboard, and tape into a life support system for a spacecraft. An outside-the-box thinker can turn a sharpened farmer's tool into a lethal weapon that could destroy a heartless enemy.

According to scholars and archaeologists, Shamgar's ox goad was tipped with an iron point and could have been as much as ten feet long since it needed to reach the rump of an ox from behind a plow. That would make it an unwieldy weapon at best, but it was all Shamgar had. We don't need the latest technology or AI super thinkers to make a difference in the world; we already have the resources of creativity and imagination.

THE POWER OF ONE

As Pat wrote in the earlier chapter, your resources include intangible assets such as your dreams, enthusiasm, talent, education, experience, influence, and wisdom. Sometimes, we focus so much on what we don't have that we overlook what we do have. People of influence are willing to lean on creativity, courage, and the promises of God. Sometimes having wealth, fame, or talent keeps us from focusing on God's ability and willingness to do *"more than you imagine."*

As the life of Shamgar shows, the most significant difference between success and failure comes down to resourcefulness. What is the talent God has given you? A talent for music, art, sports, writing, business, finance, speaking, communication, technology, a servant's heart? What about building relationships or genuine listening? My longtime friends will occasionally text or call and ask, "Have you read …... so and so…? Read it and let me know your thoughts. I just finished it," which motivates me to keep learning and growing. Those friends who have done life with me for decades give and receive the gifts of being listened to, held accountable, and sharpening one another with debates on how to impact what is happening in the world.

Pat Williams and I always lingered long over dinner to talk about life and ideas. I was significantly gifted when I walked away from our times together. I knew, and he knew, that we were there for one another any time, any place, in any situation, as we had been for the last three decades.

Pat spoke on stage with me at our SLU program the first week of the 2024 summer schedule. A few days later he called the office to say he would be out for one week but planned to return to speak the next week. Instead, Pat went into the hospital and never came out. I last visited him as he lay between heaven and earth. We prayed together, and I spoke to him and his family about heaven. As weak as he was, I saw his vitals move on the monitor and he reached for my hand in an effort to say, "I am ready." Pat went home to heaven a few days later. The legacy he left behind is living and breathing in his 19 children and the thousands he has inspired.

There have been a few challenging times in my walk with God that I lost my confidence. You may have experienced the same feeling. We daily fight against complacency, and anxiety over the unknown shakes us. This spiritual and emotional battle confronts everyone at various times in life. We may need clarification on our worldview or understanding the culture, but we don't have to live in fear. Mentors, accountability partners, and good friends who pray, listen, and do life together are part of God's plan. The resource of healthy relationships is from God, and it can't be replaced with anything else. Good friends help you win personal battles and are essential to God's plan.

THE POWER OF ONE

Ask yourself, "What am I good at? What do I enjoy doing?" Don't sell yourself short. If the Creator put a specific attribute or ability in you, it is valuable. Whatever your talent or gift, offer it back to Him and imagine unimaginable possibilities in your quiet time. If you dream 10 dreams and only one comes to a finished goal, does it matter that the nine didn't come to fruition? No, not at all, because those other nine created valuable life lessons. As the great inventor Thomas Edison said of his many tries to create the light bulb, "I have not failed. I've just found 10,000 ways that won't work."

Several years ago, a friend said, "You have to invites Julia Immonen Strachen to speak. Her story is remarkable." In my few moments of cell service while touring Normandy, France with 400 students, I asked, "Why? Who is she?" "She is a sportscaster with Sky News London who broke a world record rowing." As the phones started to break up, I said, "Send her our hotel address and we will see her tonight. Thanks, friend!" There has never been a program where I did not vet the speakers personally or through digital media, so I was a bit nervous.

Julia entered the building full of energy and began to tell her story. Like many of us, watching the film, Taken, moved her to tears for those held in human slavery. But she was more than moved in heart; she was moved to action. Raising awareness in the world of this terrorism against more than 50 million children, men, and women was her first thought. Gathering close friends and talking with her mentor, the idea of rowing with a team of women across the 3000 miles of the historic slave route from the Canary Islands to Barbados was born. Fewer people have completed this challenge than have climbed Mount Everest or gone into space. Did I mention that Julia was not a rower? But she did believe this was her call and that the Faithful God would be more than enough to make up for her lack of experience. Julia set out to raise funds, learn to row, build a team, and use her position as a sports reporter to raise awareness about this heinous crime. She is a creative thinker, a cumulative thinker.

Peril began almost the moment she decided to go for it. Her mom became ill, making Julia rethink whether she should continue. Just weeks before the trip began, the team leader dropped out. Julia, the novice rower of the team, would have to step up and lead. The seas were crossed through peril, mechanical breakdowns, huge rough waves, exhaustion, and anxiety. But as she told our students, "The setbacks bring out the gold in us. It was the most stretching time of my life. Against all odds, we made it, and I wouldn't change the challenges – crazily! One of the boats in the race was called 'Dream It, Do It.' It became my life's motto. Dreaming is easy, but the doing is tough. Life's challenges will come without a doubt, but if you don't give in to the culture of instant gratification you will make it to the other side."

THE POWER OF ONE

Not only did she finish the row, but Julia and her team broke the world record for the fastest women's crossing and established a record for being the first female crew ever to row the Atlantic. The students were mesmerized by her bravery and tenacity as was I. In her book, *Row to Freedom*, (Harper Collins) Julia challenges readers with: "We can't do everything, but we can all do something. All our somethings collectively change the world." Amen to that!

You may feel inadequate to carry out the mission God has given you. At times, you'll be staring at odds of six to one or 600-to-one, and you'll think, "What's the use! Why even try?" When that happens, I think back to the disciples Jesus chose. Not even one had a significant social standing, and all but Matthew, the hated tax collector, lived in day-by-day economics. Jesus purposely sought out each one because He saw in them the gifts He needed to build His earthly ministry. And believe it or not, He looks at you the same way.

Paul spoke of the great "thorn" in his life brought by Satan. Was it physical pain, insecurity, or great temptation? Some scholars think it was his vision. We don't know, but he prayed for the pain to be removed. The answer he received was this: *"My grace is sufficient for you, for my power is made perfect in weakness."* (2 Corinthians 12:9).

My friend, Pastor Steve Gaines, was diagnosed with myasthenia gravis. When he was called to pastor the historic Bellevue Baptist Church in Memphis, he thought about the weakness the neuromuscular disease can bring. As he prayed through the decision, the Lord gave him this verse spoken to the prophet Gideon as he faced the Midianites: *"The LORD turned to him and said, 'Go in the strength you have and save Israel out of Midian's hand. Am I not sending you?'"* Steve spoke that word to us at a pastors' conference, and I have watched him live it with grace.

The more hopeless the situation, the more dramatic God's deliverance. Sometimes, the Lord says, "Watch what I can do with just a little." In John 6, we find an instructive story: Jesus was walking beside the Sea of Galilee when a vast crowd approached him. Seeing the people, Jesus turned to one of his disciples and said, "Where shall we buy bread for these people to eat? The disciple answered, "Eight months' wages wouldn't buy enough bread for each person to have one bite!" Then another disciple brought a boy to Jesus and said, "Here's a boy with five small barley loaves and two dried, salted fish—but how far will so little food go among so many?" The answer was "As far as it needs to go..."

"Then Jesus took the loaves, gave thanks to God, and distributed them to the people. Afterward he did the same with the fish. And they all ate as much as they wanted." John 6:11 NIV

And then there was. The great King of Israel, "a man after God's own heart," who was the "runt" of his family of brothers. As far as we know, his only experience in life was being a lonely shepherd boy for his father's flock, while the brothers were given more honor.

In his young days, David was unknowingly being prepared by the Creator to step forth as a leader for the nation. How? In the simplest of ways. Day after day, he faced lions stalking the sheep and learned to protect with a rock and a slingshot. Night after night, he lay under the stars singing songs and contemplating the Lord God of the Hebrews, whose promises and power he had heard of since childhood. And daily, he prepared for unknown predators who might come his way. All of this came together to build the shepherd boy's creative, courageous mind.

Though these events occurred some four hundred years after Shamgar, the enemies and odds were the same. The narrative of Shamgar may have multiplied David's courage. The Philistines gathered their forces for war on one hill and the Israelites on another, with the valley between them.

The progression of the story in 1 Samuel 17 is fascinating. Daily, for 40 days, the Philistine giant taunted the Israelites with enslavement and death, but David wasn't there to hear it. He was back in the hills picking up lunch for his brothers, who were waiting along with the terrified army of Israelites. The story reads like an animated short – the boy runs across the hill with food, sees the battle lines drawn, and the giant Goliath roaring. He looks around to see what's going on, hears the taunting message, and asks, "What does one get for killing this guy?" His brother rebukes him as wicked and commands him to return home. So, David sits, watches, considers, and thinks. No one is moving. Fear permeates the hills. And then he walks up to King Saul and says, "Let me do it." He proceeds to give his resume: "I kill lions and bears because the living God has rescued me. He will do it today as well." In all of Israel, only one was willing to go up against the odds of defeating Goliath— He wasn't even a soldier. In a preposterous move, a King agreed to send an untrained boy. Perhaps he was using David as a sacrificial lamb to gain a little time.

They tried to dress David up in armor, but he declined, sticking to "what I am used to." Now, this is an important point – get this. We talk over and over about preparation in life, but we are not talking about preparation for a test, an interview, or an event. Keep that point in mind as we speak of preparation. Learning to use the slingshot and stones was never intended for a giant enemy, but he practiced and became good enough to use it skillfully in any situation. David allowed his creative "out of the box" thinking to devise a way no one else had thought of or even considered.

This confidence in the power of the living Lord was his greatest weapon, just as it is our greatest weapon

THE POWER OF ONE

in the daily battles of life. *"Then he took his staff in his hand, chose five smooth stones from the stream, put them in the pouch of his shepherd's bag and, with his sling in his hand, approached the Philistine."* (1 Sam 17:40). Why five stones instead of one? In case Goliath had brothers lurking nearby, he was ready. David thought both cumulatively and creatively.

When the moment came, *"David sprinted toward the battle line to meet him."* (v. 48) I have stood on this battlefield many, many times and even today the magnitude of danger is felt. It is a real place; the event happened to real people. God did come through powerfully. As much as this story inspires, it also points out how little we may be preparing or looking for opportunities. It may feel like your efforts go unnoticed or seem unimportant; but every day is an important day; every day carries a lesson learned.

Stronger than his skill was the preparation of his soul from childhood and beyond. Hearing the promises of God is a start; believing them enough to be filled with valor is quite another.

The stone struck deep into Goliath's forehead. The Philistine fell like—well, like a stone.

The story's point is that God wants us to use what we have, even if it's just an ox goad or five smooth stones. God has given us all the resources we need to gain victory over the Philistines in our lives.

Every day, all around us, there are Goliath-sized enemies who are bigger, meaner, and far more powerful than we are. You and I may face all kinds of gigantic challenges, obstacles, opponents, losses, failures, and temptations, but not one of them is a match for the plan, purpose, and power of the Living God.

We've looked at two Old Testament stories that show how God uses creative approaches to even the odds and win the battle. In the story of Shamgar, we see that God used an unlikely hero—a farmer armed only with an ox goad—to defeat a vastly superior enemy. In the story of David and Goliath, we see God using the same approach differently: instead of a farmer with an ox goad, he uses a boy with a sling and some stones.

Do you see a pattern emerging? In the New Testament, Paul explained God's creative method this way: *"But God chose the foolish things of the world to shame the wise; God chose the weak things of the world to shame the strong."* (1 Cor. 1:27).

You may think, "Well, that was then, but this is now. God doesn't work that way anymore." If that's what you're thinking, you are wrong! God still uses weak, foolish, and unlikely people like us to accomplish His purposes. As Paul wrote in 2 Corinthians 12:10, *"That is why, for Christ's sake, I delight in weaknesses, in insults, in hardships, persecutions, in difficulties. For when I am weak, then I am strong."*

THE POWER OF ONE

When God calls us to a task or mission, He also enables, prepares, and equips us. The beauty of the worship throughout the Psalms began when the boy lay under the stars singing to the one Who created the stars. We may feel we are over our heads, but we are never alone in a challenge. You have the promises and truths of Scripture; you have the Holy Spirit of God living within you; and you have the declaration of 1 John 4:4 NIV, *"You, dear children, are from God and have overcome them, because the One who is in you is greater than the one who is in the world."* Even if we fail or think we have disappointed God and everyone around us, His truths and power still hold.

I know that feeling of being unnoticed, without direction, and insecure. As a new Christian, I knew God loved me, but I had no idea how to move forward. Was there a "next" for an ex-junkie? Most of my high school years were spent in a drug-induced haze, sitting in the back row, just barely getting by. All of that changed after my life-changing encounter with Jesus Christ—thanks to Charlie's prayers and persistent witness.

After years of dyslexia and skipping school, I suddenly wanted to learn more about this God and His book that changed my life. Week after week, I attended the Bible study where I first heard the Good News, listened actively, took notes, and paid attention. Life was new, but it felt just too good to be true. The Bible studies of the Jesus movement gave me a foundation, but as those started to wane, I knew I needed more. There was a Christian bookstore in the area where I ambled about the aisles almost daily. One day the older gentleman who owned the place approached with a smile, "Can I help you find something?" I wanted to say, "Yes," but I had no idea what I was looking for. We became friends over the weeks, and after I explained my focus and reading challenges, he recommended the Stetson University Extension class called "Old Testament Survey." I scarcely knew that the Bible was divided into an Old and New Testament, but he said I could audit the course without qualifying. For me, it was a miracle.

The professor was Dr. H. Fred Williams, a pastor, and father of four. With gray hair, a matching gray suit, a white shirt, black shoes, and a narrow tie, he looked as much a part of the "establishment" as I looked a part of the hippie counterculture. I tried to sneak by his desk, afraid he might just clear his throat and say, "I don't think so." But Dr. Fred looked past my hair and ignorance of the Bible. From the moment he smiled, "Welcome," I felt comfortable. He seemed to genuinely care as he listened and answered my questions.

He taught the story of Shamgar, and the Holy Spirit lit a fire in me. Over the next few weeks, the Shamgar principles filled my mind, and I'd think, "Start where you are." Where was I? I might be at the checkout stand at the grocery store or on the steps of the library. "Use what you have." I had a story—my own story about how I had first encountered Jesus. "Do what you can." Well, I could tell my story. So that's what I did. Wherever I happened to be, I began telling my story to anyone and everyone who might be in earshot. Some people walked away. Others ran away. Some stayed and listened. A few considered what I had to say, and they received Christ as Savior.

When asked to pastor the tiny church congregation, I felt completely unqualified. I had only attended church a few times, yet these people wanted me to be their pastor! What should I do? Then I remembered that I had prayed and asked God to use me and work through my life. I decided to start where I was, a tiny church with a group of people who wanted me to be there. How could I say no?

Week after week, I got up in the pulpit of that tiny church and preached sermons in my stumbling way. I repeatedly went to Dr. Fred for advice and encouragement, and he patiently mentored and discipled me. I didn't have the skills, knowledge, or educational background to do such a thing; I knew it was God doing the work.

As it turned out, that was just the beginning of an adventure that has continued for decades. The kid who once got kicked out of the classroom has had the privilege of speaking in schools and universities, walking into boardrooms of leading corporations, sharing the stage with national politicians, and delivering messages of inspiration and motivation to professional sports teams. Once turned down by thirteen colleges, the kid has now addressed the faculty and students at several universities and founded Student Leadership University and the Center for Global Leadership at Charleston Southern University. The kid nobody would pay attention to has now shared the name of Jesus with thousands of audiences totaling more than millions of people. Through it all, I remain keenly aware that – *"God has chosen the foolish things of this world..."* 1 Cor 1:27

Dr. H. Fred Williams looked at me one day and said, "Jay, God wants to use you. He wants to work through you to demonstrate his power to other people. And all you have to do is be available."

Right now, you may be thinking of someone who needs you to listen, encourage, and love them unconditionally. Plan now to do just that by deciding what day you will reach out to that person this week. Perhaps you need those same gifts yourself. The principles of Shamgar work 100% of the time, but we have no idea what the result will be except that God does *"more than we can imagine."* (Ephesians 3:20 The Message)

Pat Williams and I became close friends by chance. Coming out of the Orlando Magic shop in downtown Orlando, I saw Pat in the parking lot and approached him. We had spoken at events before and knew each

THE POWER OF ONE

other from afar. That day, I asked him, "How can I pray for you?" At that particular moment, Pat needed prayer for a personal situation. We prayed there in front of Magic fans in the parking lot and that was the beginning of a special friendship. One thing I remember about Pat is that he never stopped learning. At every Magic game, I watched him stand in the press aisle reading a book. And no matter his fame, he was in church and in small group Bible study every Sunday he was in town. He was one of a kind.

One evening over dinner, Pat said, "Jay-Bird, I want you to speak at the chapel for the NBA All-Stars before the game in New York." I knew it would be held at Madison Square Garden and that many of my favorite players would be there. "Yes" came out of my mouth so fast that I almost choked on my food.

The NBA All-Star Game takes place halfway through the basketball season. Players are chosen based on the individual's performance and popularity, regardless of how well or how poorly their teams are doing. Some players come from teams heading for the playoffs, others from teams struggling to reach 500.

Midway through the season, players sometimes become complacent. When winning, they may be tempted to settle instead of striving for what could be. When losing, they might think about giving up for what looks like an inevitable loss. A mindset of mediocrity can easily set in. But for those struggling at midseason, it's not too late for that team to turn on the heat and make a run for the playoffs—and it's also not too late for a dominant team to become smug and sloppy and lose that winning edge.

I began the chapel by asking the players: "What can you do to turn this season around for your team? What can one person do? Are you settling into a rut of complacency? Or are you making the most of every opportunity?" I wanted them to think, "I can be the one person to turn an ordinary team into a championship team. I can beat the odds."

As Shamgar's story unfolded to these guys about a man who saved an entire nation, armed only with an ox goad, I shared the same three principles I first heard in Dr. Williams' Old Testament Survey class: "Shamgar won the battle because he started where he was, used what he had, and did what he could."

I could see the eyes of the players light up when they heard those three principles. The story of Shamgar made sense to these men whose entire careers required striving, competing, and struggling to win. The simple, short story of Shamgar made sense. I knew the principles could transform lives because they dramatically altered my life. I explained that I and many others admired them because of the odds they had already overcome - the injuries, vital shots missed, or slow starts. I also reminded the players that their fame could influence a community, a neighborhood, or a city block. My story was simple, but one many of them could relate to.

After the chapel was over, Pat said, "Jay, that was a great message. I can't wait to read the book!" I laughed and said, "Pat, there are only two verses about Shamgar." The next time we had dinner together, I told Pat I was thinking about writing a book about the Shamgar principles. He replied, "I already started it!" It was then that we came together to write this book, and it has been fun.

I hope you are thinking, "OK, if Jay can overcome all of his crazy background, I can overcome mine." That is my prayer for every person I encounter, and it is what keeps me going on the road, getting on the plane, picking up the phone, or sharing over Zoom. If I can do it, indeed anyone can.

Be Inspired Every Day

God continued through the ups and downs to bring the story of Shamgar to my life. It was following me at one point. Sitting on the stage, waiting my turn to preach, it was my privilege to share the platform with Dr. E. V. Hill, one of my most memorable spiritual heroes. I was still new to this preaching stuff and unprepared for the intense passion that poured out of this man. As he presented his sermon, I listened earnestly, mesmerized by every word. That day, Dr. Hill spoke about Shamgar—this same obscure judge of ancient Israel I had first heard about from Dr Williams. While Dr. Fred had taught me the principles in his wise, warm, quiet manner, Dr. Hill pounded them into my heart with thunder and lightning. To this day, he remains one of the most powerful preachers I have ever heard. I can still hear his voice ringing in my memory: "Shamgar did what he could, with what he had, right where he was—and every chance he got!"

I was glad to have shared my testimony before he spoke because I sat in quiet awe after his message. After the event, I spent a few minutes with this great man of God and commented on how much his message impacted me. Dr. Hill shook my hand and said, "Jay, what you have is a testimony of God's grace. You swing that testimony like Shamgar swung the ox goad and watch what God will do." A light bulb went off in my head. All the abuse, mistakes, and shame would now become a powerful tool. For 40 years and counting, I have been swinging my ox goad and watching what God continues to do.

Who was E. V. Hill to put so much energy and focus into preaching such a crazy story as Shamgar? Why would he choose that obscure passage from all the great stories of the ancients? E. V. was a guy like me, someone like you, who triumphed over obstacles and adversity in life. As I heard E.V. tell it, the story of Edward Victor Hill began in a little log cabin in southeast Texas during the Great Depression. "Mamma" was a

THE POWER OF ONE

woman who was not related biologically but who raised E.V. When he was eleven years old, she led him in a prayer to give his life to Jesus Christ.

One day, Mamma stood up in church and told the congregation, "My boy E. V. is going to finish high school." It was an unusual prophecy for those Depression-era days. Most African American boys left school out of necessity to find jobs. But E.V. did graduate, just as Mamma said he would. She went further and promised E. V. that he would go to college—and that was even more unheard of. When he graduated high school, Mamma bought him new clothes and gave him five dollars for the new life ahead. At the bus station, her goodbye was, "I'll be praying for you." E.V. bought his ticket, boarded the bus, and arrived at the campus of Prairie View A&M with $1.58 left in his pocket. Ed Hill got in line to register for classes, only to be met by a sign informing all new students of a $83 cash payment at registration. He was about to step out of line and walk away when he heard Mamma's voice in his mind, saying, "I'll be praying for you." He figured he had nothing to lose by standing in line a few minutes longer. When he reached the front line and gave his name, the registrar said, "You're Ed Hill? Our office has been trying to contact you. The university wants to offer you a four-year scholarship—tuition, room and board, and a $35-a-month expense allowance." Again, he remembered Mamma's words: "I'll be praying for you."[18]

As fantastic as that true story is, there is a "middle" story with a significant point. E. V. began preaching after college, but the church couldn't pay him enough to live on. He pooled together what little money he could and bought a service station. Within months, the business went broke, and Hill lost his investment.

Why is this important? Because at a pivotal time in his life, E. V. Hill could have stopped and said, "I failed. I am done trying." He could have easily given up and stopped reaching for dreams. Instead of living in the "safe zone," E.V. went on to pastor the Mount Zion Missionary Baptist Church in the heart of the troubled Watts section of south-central Los Angeles. He served there for 42 years, gaining the respect of everyone from businesses to street gangs and frequently mediating disputes between rival factions. He even spearheaded a street-level peace movement called "The Moratorium on Gang Murder."

Under his leadership, Mount Zion became a hub of political activism and social compassion in the center of Los Angeles. E. V. Hill transcended distinctions of left and right and the turmoil of race relations that day and instead focused on bringing people together.

There weren't many opportunities for a young black man in southeast Texas during the Great Depression. Still, E.V. Hill lived by Mamma's prophetic prayers and became a friend of the poor in spirit and a counselor to Presidents. If he had given up that day at the service station, he would not have marched with Dr. Martin Luther King and demanded that justice roll down like mighty waters. He probably would not have fed the hungry and brought peace to warring neighborhoods. And he would not have shared the refreshing message of Jesus with thirsty souls. But he did all those things because E. V. Hill dared to live in the realm of possibility.

Creativity is Our Birthright

Some may remember a famous blues rock band from England's 1960s rock and roll scene. My wife came to Christ at one of their concerts. Looking about at the sin that surrounded her, she thought, "There has to be more to life than this. Jesus, here is my life." She has never been the same. Our God is creative in reaching out to us any way He can to grab our attention.

The band was hot in their time, but few knew that the name came from a pioneering farmer-inventor of a previous era. The original Jethro Tull was born in Berkshire, England in 1674. He was an ordinary farmer who created one of human history's most notable agricultural revolutions. As Tull planted the fields one seed at a time, he mused there had to be an easier way to grow a few acres of corn. He let his imagination run through ideas as he rummaged through the toolshed of rusting parts.

Discarded pieces of an old pipe organ caught his attention. Tull tinkered with the pieces, eventually devising a machine that could dispense seed three rows at once by way of a rotating cylinder. From there, he kept imagining until he invented a drill that made holes in the earth. Jethro's seed drill quickly became a widely used labor saving tool that dramatically increased crop yields in Europe and America.[19]

One thing I noted from this story when I first read it is that Tull gave intentional hours to thinking. That might be because there was little else to do in the 1600s as a farmer. In contrast, in our modern lives, the plethora of choices, diversions, entertainment, and social interactions keep us from deep thinking and intentional dreaming. Choose every day where your thoughts will go and who will control them. Music, media, digital, relationships – all of these may attempt to control. Don't be afraid to turn it all off and sit before the Lord as you think. A lack of resources is the least of the roadblocks in our lives.

The lesson is clear: You can do a lot with a little if you are willing to be creative. Let me take it down to a simple illustration you can easily visualize. My grandson loves to fish, as do all his siblings. Gabe was excited to use his new pole and a colorful lure in our lake behind the house. His sister, Charis, was not happy that he had the only pole at the house, so she started rummaging through the garage for fishing gear. Her ever-stirring creativity reminded her of a big, heavy stick she once stashed on the side of the house. Together with a piece of leftover line that Gabe had dropped and some stale bread on a hook, she created a fishing pole of sorts.

Charis made her way confidently down to the dock where her brother was laughing at the feeble invention. Not to be deterred, Charis stood alongside Gabe and waited. Not long after, we heard a loud "whoop" and exhilaration along the waterfront. Gabe hadn't caught a thing with his new pole, but Charis had a big bass on her stick. We took pictures, teased Gabe, and laughed about that one for a while. And now and then at a family dinner, we will laugh at the story and remind everyone of the creativity of Charis. As I wrote earlier, lack of resources is not the problem; lack of resourcefulness is.

I am asking you to focus on one thing every day: Creativity is your birthright planted within you by the Creator God. Don't say, "If only" you had updated technology, better tools, or more money to serve God and achieve your goals. You were created by the One who fashioned animals, nature, and humanity by thinking and speaking it. If you allow your creativity the time to think, if that is an integral part of your days, you will achieve remarkable results with whatever resources you have.

When I think of creativity, I'm reminded of a student who attended one of our first Student Leadership University programs at the age of 16 as a junior in high school. Her name is Nikki Finch Hoffpauir. While a junior in high school, Nikki began to pray for God to use her efforts to make a difference in the world. She decided she would not be stopped by age, gender, circumstance, or closed doors. In her words,

"I first grasped what could happen in my life if I would simply believe what Philippians 4:13 tells me: "I can do everything through [Christ] who gives me strength" In one session, Dr. Strack looked each student in the eye and asked, "If you had no limits on your life, what would you do? What goals would you set for your life?" He gave us ten minutes to write down our thoughts. Some students wrote that they would lose weight, read more, or try harder in school. Good goals but I told myself, Nikki, think big! Dr. Strack said, 'No limits" What would that be like—living life without limits?

I wrote down that I would like to meet the President of the United States. Then I wrote that I would like to work undercover for the CIA. Lastly, I wrote that I would like to be a national speaker for SADD, Students Against Drunk Driving.

When I read my goals aloud, some thought they were unreachable. Yet, what I learned at SLU was that nothing is unreachable when we as believers stop putting limits on what God can do through us. And while, if I am honest, I wrote those goals thinking they would happen 'someday,' but I soon learned that God does not

THE POWER OF ONE

have an age minimum on those He works through. He is ready as soon as we start taking Him seriously.

Though I still haven't gotten an assignment from the CIA, yet, I was selected, within a year of writing these goals, to be the National SADD Student of the Year. I traveled around the country speaking out on alcohol abuse and the positive difference students can make in the lives of their peers. Reaching that goal led to another - I met with the President of the United States at the White House to discuss with him as a representative of SADD to push for a national blood alcohol standard of .08. With the encouragement of family, friends, and mentors, we then set our sights on a new alcohol abuse issue. I teamed up with New York's attorney general, Dennis Vacco, to end the practice of selling alcohol to minors over the Internet. I helped set up sting operations and lobbied Congress for federal legislation. We stood toe to toe with the alcohol industry and won. Over the course of the next eight years, I traveled to twenty-six states and three countries, speaking out on health and safety issues that affect my peers. I've held over forty press conferences, from the Capitol building to the White House, and I've appeared on news programs from NBC's Today Show to CNN. I've met with President Clinton, lobbied Congress, and sat on the boards of directors of three national nonprofit organizations. I earned a bachelor's degree from Florida State and spent a year serving the D.C. inner-city schools with

AmeriCorps before going on to receive my M.A. from George Washington University in D.C.

I attended SLU more than two decades ago as a student. Today I am the COO of Student Leadership University and have the opportunity to pour into students across the globe. Students can make a difference in the world if they will open their minds and hearts to believe that God will do the impossible if they will do the possible."

It is a fact - anyone can make a difference in the world if they are willing to risk, sacrifice, think, plan, and gather teams. All it takes is an open and creative mind, faith that God can do anything, and the courage to stay the course until the goal is reached.

SIX

Your Life Mission

- Pat Williams

"Strive not to be a success, but rather to be of value."
Albert Einstein

"The world is a mess, but what can one person do?"

You've heard words like those before. But as you have been reading, one person *can change the world*—or at least a little piece of it.

One person can share a word of encouragement or a smile with another person who desperately needs it. One person can give an hour or a day or a lifetime to a worthy cause. One person can adopt a child or mentor a troubled teen. One person can speak up and defend another person who is being treated unjustly. One person can show love and forgiveness instead of hatred and bitterness.

Think of it this way: Somewhere there is a vitally important task that no one is doing. If you don't do it, then it simply won't get done. You are essential to God's plan. If you do not carry out the life mission God has given you, your work will simply go undone.

April 21, 1855, a Bible teacher named Edward Kimball walked into Holton's Shoe Store in Boston. He saw a young shoe clerk wrapping shoes, and without even a word of introduction, he said to the clerk, "Young man, I want to tell you how much Jesus Christ loves you." The clerk listened, and Mr. Kimball talked. After a while, the young clerk got down on his knees and prayed, asking Jesus Christ to become the Lord of his life. That young clerk's name was Dwight L. Moody.

Moody became an evangelist and preached across the United States. In 1879, he went to England and held a series of evangelistic meetings there. One of those who came to hear Moody was a pastor named Fredrick B. Meyer. Prior to hearing Moody speak, Meyer believed that his purpose in life was to (as he put it) "increase my influence, make money, draw audiences and do philanthropic work." He didn't believe in the reality of a living, dynamic God who was truly involved in human lives.

All of that changed when Meyer heard Dwight L. Moody speak. The English pastor went to his knees and surrendered his life to Jesus Christ, and his ministry in the church was forever transformed. F. B. Meyer became a great preacher and author who influenced thousands of people to make a life-changing decision for Jesus Christ.

Meyer came to the United States and preached to packed auditoriums throughout New England and down the Atlantic coast. One of those who heard Meyer preach

THE POWER OF ONE

was J. Wilbur Chapman. Chapman's soul was so stirred by the Gospel that he decided to become an evangelist like F. B. Meyer.

J. Wilbur Chapman became involved with several Christian ministries, including an organization that merged the Christian Gospel with athletics, the Young Men's Christian Association (YMCA).

Through the YMCA, Chapman became acquainted with a former pro baseball player named Billy Sunday. Billy Sunday had played for National League clubs in Chicago, Pittsburgh, and Philadelphia in the late 1800s, and was the first player to run the bases in fourteen seconds. In 1886, he asked Jesus to be the Lord of his life through an outreach of the Pacific Garden Mission in Chicago. Five years later, he quit baseball (turning down salary offers that would have paid him more money per week than most people made in a year). Billy Sunday joined J. Wilbur Chapman's evangelistic organization, becoming a preacher and evangelist.

One place where Billy Sunday's preaching had a special impact was Charlotte, North Carolina. A group of Charlotte businessmen were so deeply impacted by Billy Sunday's ministry that they organized a committee to bring evangelists to Charlotte on a regular basis. One of the evangelists they invited was Mordecai Ham of Louisville, Kentucky.

In 1934, during one of Mordecai Ham's evangelistic meetings, there was a troubled young man sitting in the audience who was struggling with giving his heart to God. At the end of the service, that young man walked forward and prayed to ask Jesus Christ to take control of his life. That young man's name was Billy Graham.

No one knows for sure how many people Billy Graham has preached to in tents, auditoriums, and stadiums over the years, but it is estimated at over a billion. And as his ministry lives on through his son, Franklin Graham, and the thousands upon thousands of volunteers and staff of both the Billy Graham Association and Samaritan's Purse. There is no sign of those ministries ever declining, and the number of people served and saved becomes impossible to calculate.

What can one person do? I doubt that Edward Kimball had any idea the chain of events he was setting in motion that day he told a young shoe clerk about the love of Jesus Christ. No one ever knows the long-range impact their words or actions may have. All we know is that we must start where we are, use what we have and do what we can—then leave the rest to God. Someday in eternity we may look back and be amazed at what those few words of ours ultimately accomplished.

Shamgar did what he could, and he saved a nation. If you don't think you're up to saving a nation, then start a little smaller. Save a child. Save a tree. Save a whale. You can't do everything, but you can do something.

THE POWER OF ONE

Let me suggest seven things you can do that can make a difference in your life and the lives of people around you. Do these seven things and you just might change the world.

Pray

Most of us think of prayer as a last resort, an act of desperation: "If all else fails, pray." But if we realized the true power and effectiveness of prayer, we would probably spend half our days on our knees. As Charles H. Spurgeon once said, "Prayer is the slender nerve that moves the muscle of Omnipotence."

Minister and devotional writer E. M. Bounds described prayer this way: "God shapes the world by prayer. Prayers are deathless. The lips that uttered them may be closed in death, the heart that felt them may have ceased to beat, but their prayers live before God, and God's heart is set on them. Prayers outlive the lives of those who uttered them; outlive a generation; outlive an age; outlive a world."

Bill Bright, the late founder of Campus Crusade for Christ and a man I was honored to know as a friend, once described prayer this way: "It is impossible to overexaggerate the importance of prayer: 'Whatever you ask in my name,' Jesus said, 'I will do it.' And whatever we ask, according to God's will, he will hear and answer. These are promises."

English preacher and author J. Sidlow Baxter put prayer in perspective when he wrote, "Men may spurn our appeals, reject our message, oppose our arguments, or despise our persons, but they are helpless against our prayers." And Oswald Chambers, author of *My Utmost for His Highest*, said, "Prayer does not equip us for greater works. Prayer *is* the greater work."

How, then, should we pray? Are there specific components or steps to effective prayer? I believe there are. Based on my own experience with prayer, I would suggest these steps to an effective prayer life:

First, *start your day with prayer*. Oswald Chambers once said, "If in the first waking moment of the day you learn to fling the door back and let God in, every public thing will be stamped with the presence of God." As you greet the day, greet God. Ask him to walk with you throughout the day.

Second, *pray unceasingly*. Paul, in 1 Thessalonians 5:17, says, *"Pray continually."* You might think it's impossible to pray continually and unceasingly, but it's not. Every conversation between friends has its pauses, its quiet moments. So does prayer. Your conversation with God may have pauses that last a half hour, an hour, or more, but the conversation goes on. When you rise in the morning, as you stare glassy-eyed into your first cup of coffee, as you drive to work, as you pause to say thanks for your lunch, as you face a crisis at the office, as you drive home, as you greet your loved ones at the

THE POWER OF ONE

door, as you have dinner, as you relax before bedtime, as your head sinks into the pillow—Talk to God. Listen to God. Remain in a warm, friendly, day long, lifelong, unceasing conversation with your heavenly Friend, the Maker of the Universe, the Maker of you. He's available and he's listening, 24/7. You'll probably find that the more you pray, the more you want to pray. You won't want to be out of his presence, his sight, his earshot, even for a moment.

Third, *pray from the heart*. Honestly tell God what you are thinking and feeling. Don't worry about using all the right religious words. You don't need to pray in King James English; just talk to God as you would talk to a close friend, to a loving Father. He doesn't care about your memorized phrases or religious clichés—he just wants to hear what's on your mind. Plus, he wants you to hear what's on his mind.

Praying from the heart also means: Don't hold back. Are you angry with God? Tell him. Yell if you need to. He can take it. He'd rather receive your honest feelings from the top of your lungs than to hear nothing but a chilly silence. If something good happens, and you feel grateful and joyful, tell him that, too. He'd love to hear about it. Nothing you say is going to shock God or make him turn his back on you. He loves you more than you love yourself.

Fourth, *pray specifically*. Tell God exactly how you feel, and exactly what you need, and exactly what you hope for. Sure, he already knows what we need. He knows our hopes and dreams. Tell him anyway. He likes to hear it from us.

When praying specifically, *expect an answer.* Remember, his answer might be "No," or "Not yet." Why? Because just as children sometimes ask for things that their parents know are not the best for them, we sometimes ask for one thing when God has something better in mind. Even though God sometimes says "No" to our prayers, you'd be surprised at how often he says "Yes!" Like any loving parent, God would much rather say "Yes" to his children than "No." So pray specifically and watch for his answers. Better yet, keep a prayer journal and write down the requests you make— followed by the date that your request was answered. I guarantee that if you keep a journal of your prayers and God's answers, you'll be amazed, and your faith will soar.

Fifth, *pray boldly and confidently.* The New Testament book of Hebrews tells us, "Let us then approach the throne of grace with confidence, so that we may receive mercy and find grace to help us in our time of need" (Heb. 4:16). Understand, I'm not saying that we should order God around or make demands of him. We need to pray with humility. But we should also go to God with confidence, knowing that he is merciful and gracious, and he wants to answer our prayers.

THE POWER OF ONE

Jesus said, "So I say to you: Ask and it will be given to you; seek and you will find; knock and the door will be opened to you. For everyone who asks receives; he who seeks finds; and to him who knocks, the door will be opened" (Luke 11:9–10). In short, Jesus is saying that we should pray boldly and confidently, expecting God to act on our prayers. That is an ironclad promise from Jesus himself.

Sixth, *pray audibly*. You may have noticed that when you pray silently, "thinking" your prayers to God, your mind tends to wander, you get distracted—and you may even fall asleep! I guarantee that you won't fall asleep if you pray out loud.

You may feel a little odd at first when you pray aloud—you might feel as if you are talking to yourself. But there's something about talking audibly to God that enables you to focus, to pray with enthusiasm and intensity. Find a place where you can go to be alone, a place of solitude where you won't be overheard. Make that your refuge, your sanctuary, where you can genuinely, honestly speak with and listen to your God.

Seventh, *pray obediently*. Someone once said, "When you pray, don't give God instructions. Just report for duty." We should come to God with an obedient mind-set, ready not only to present our requests to him, but also to receive our orders from him. If God is truly Lord of our lives, then we must come to him humbly and obediently, willing to go where he sends us and do what he asks us to do.

Many people are afraid to approach God this way. They fear God's will. They are afraid that God will ask them to do what they are afraid to do. And sometimes it's true that God will, out of his great love for us, ask us to move beyond our comfort zone to serve him and others. We must pray for courage to face our fears and to obediently do God's will.

Pastor and author Max Lucado once wrote, "How did Jesus endure the terror of the crucifixion? He went, first, to the Father with his fears. He modeled the words of Psalm 56:3: - "When I am afraid, I put my trust in you" (NLT). Do the same with yours. Don't avoid life's Gardens of Gethsemane. Enter them. Just don't enter them alone."

Eighth, *pray collectively*. Join your prayers with the prayers of others. Jesus said, "Again, I tell you that if two of you on earth agree about anything you ask for, it will be done for you by my Father in heaven. For where two or three come together in my name, there am I with them" (Matt. 18:19–20). Certainly, God hears us when we pray to him one on one. But something special happens when two or more believers join their hearts and agree together in prayer.

Linebacker Peter Boulware of the Baltimore Ravens once said, "Prayer is like breathing to me. It is the key to life; it's talking to the Lord. It's not only me praying, but I have a lot of people praying for me, and I pray for other people."

Ninth, *pray forgivingly*. When Jesus taught his disciples to pray, he told them to say, "Forgive us our sins, for we also forgive everyone who sins against us" (Luke 11:4). Forgiveness is a critical component of effective prayer. A spirit of bitterness or anger blocks prayer; forgiveness keeps the channel of God's grace open and flowing.

NHL star Markus Naslund of the Vancouver Canucks recalls, "I was helping at a Christian hockey camp. One of the kids asked me about my coach, and I said, 'I'm not too fond of him.' Later, a lady came up to me and said 'Why don't you try this: Don't say anything negative about your coach. Just pray for him every day.' I thought, 'Yeah, I might as well. It's tough to dislike someone when you're praying for them.' I started praying for my coach every day, and I felt a big stone lift off my heart. It was cool to see how the relationship has built up. My coach started playing me more and respecting me. In the end, we were like good friends."

Tenth, *leave the results* to God. Tony Dungy, head coach of the Indianapolis Colts, said, "With anything that comes across my desk, if I pray about it and ask for the Lord's direction, he's going to work those situations for his glory. It will be for the best, and it will succeed—maybe not the success the world would see, but success in his eyes."

It's true. What looks like success to God often looks like failure to the world. When Jesus prayed in the Garden of Gethsemane and asked to be spared the horrors of the cross, God the Father answered "No." So Jesus obediently submitted himself to the will of the Father.

The Roman soldiers nailed him to a wooden cross and suspended him between the earth and sky. There, he died. To everyone who watched him die, Jesus looked like an absolute failure. But God knew that the death of Jesus would produce success beyond anyone's ability to imagine.

So it is with us and our prayers. We must pray. We must ask for God's direction. We must trust him to work in all the situations of our lives. And we must leave the results to him. Those results will always be successful results in God's eyes—but they may not look like success to us, or to the people around us. None of that matters. Our job is to keep praying and trusting.

However, God chooses to answer prayer, it will be a success in his eyes, even if it looks like failure from a human perspective. Never assume that God didn't answer your prayer. Don't assume that he's gone back on his promises. Rest in His love for you, leave the results to him, and wait to see how the next stage of his plan for your life unfolds. Keep praying, keep listening, keep trusting.

THE POWER OF ONE

Think

Before you take any action, first pray, then think. A surgeon was once asked, "If you only had five minutes to perform a lifesaving operation, what would you do?" His answer: "I would spend the first three minutes thinking and planning the procedure."

In a crisis, people often neglect to stop and think. "It's an emergency!" they say. "I have to act! I don't have time to think!" They don't realize that acting without thinking is likely to make the problem worse, not better. Thinking time is never wasted time. Time spent thinking through all the possibilities may be the most productive thing you do.

Think about your problems in a focused, effective, and productive way: First, *think deliberately.* When faced with a problem or a crisis, don't just let your mind whirl around in a dither. Slow down. Take a deep breath. Get focused and centered. Think carefully, logically, and deliberately about the situation. Analyze the issues. Clarify your goals. Plan your strategy. Ask yourself questions to help reveal the sources and solutions of your problem, such as:

- "What is the problem?" You can't begin solving the problem until you have clearly defined and understood the nature of the problem.
- "What is the source or cause of the problem?" At this point, you're not trying to

fix blame; you're trying to fix the problem. So don't ask, "Whose fault is it?" Ask, "Where did this problem originate? What are the possible causes?"

- "What are the possible solutions?" Most problems don't have just one solution, but a range of potential solutions. Be creative. Explore a range of alternatives before settling on one single solution to the problem.

- "What are the downsides of the various solutions?" Are there undesirable side effects to some possible solutions? This will help to eliminate unworkable solutions and narrow your range of options.

- "What resources do I need to solve the problem?" Some solutions may turn out, on examination, to be too expensive to implement. Others might be easily and cheaply implemented with the resources you have on hand. This question, too, will help you to narrow your range of options down to the one or two best solutions.

- "What is my decision?" Having followed the first five steps of this process, you will probably find that the final step is an easy one. Careful step-by-step thinking makes the decision-making process easier and more effective.

Second, *think flexibly*. Never allow your mind to be set in concrete. Most problems have multiple solutions, and the best solution is often the least expected. As events change, as new information comes our way, we must always be ready to change our plans and revise our thinking. We must be nimble and responsive to every new and unexpected contingency that pops up in front of us. If a door slams shut in our faces, we need to open a window, scramble through, and keep moving toward our goals.

Inventor Edwin Land once said, "New ideas are easy. Getting rid of the old ones is hard." To clear your mind of rusty, outmoded ideas, you must develop a habit of thinking flexibly. There's no doubt in my mind that Shamgar must have had a flexible, agile mind. In the process of knocking off an army of 600 Philistine invaders, he probably discovered fifty-seven ways of using an ox goad that he had never thought of before.

Third, *think logically* and with precision. Sloppy thinking produces costly mistakes. Make a habit of checking everything twice. Be conscientious about thinking clearly, being sure of your facts, and using sound, logical reasoning in arriving at your conclusions.

Fourth, *think systematically*. Use a thinking system that works. Here are some suggestions for a systematic approach to thinking:

- Set aside a daily, regular time (ideally, at least half an hour) for intense, focused thinking. Combine your thinking time with prayer time. Use this time for brainstorming new ideas or analyzing a problem.
- Focus your thinking on your life mission, the grand goals you feel called to accomplish in your life, and the steps you must take to achieve those goals. Don't waste time thinking about trivialities. Don't daydream. Focus on what is truly important in your life.

Use pencil and paper, a journal or diary, or a computer to make your thoughts tangible and to provide a written record of your thought processes.

- Set aside a specific place that is your thinking place—a room or a park or a rooftop where you can go and focus your thoughts without interruption. Leave your phone behind and enter your sanctuary of thought.

Systematic thinking is powerful, effective thinking. Once you learn to think systematically and regularly, you will begin to see enormous acceleration in your progress toward your goals.

Fifth, *think big!* Think grand, bold, audacious thoughts. Brainstorm ideas and solutions that are so wild and startling that people will think you're crazy. When you successfully implement your big, bold ideas, people will think you're a genius! Great accomplishments are always preceded by great thoughts and great ideas. Don't be timid. Think big!!

Set Goals

If you want to succeed like Shamgar, you must set goals, then move toward those goals in a deliberate and determined way. Goals give direction to your life. Goals enable you to chart your progress on the journey to your destination—the fulfillment of your life's mission. Goals give direction and purpose to life. If you have no goals, you are just marking time until you die.

John Maxwell once said, "Ninety-five percent of achieving anything is knowing what you want and paying the price to get it." Having clear goals is the best way to determine if you are making good use of your time. Whenever you engage in a certain activity, you can ask yourself:

"Does this activity move me toward my goals—or does it keep me from my goals?"

The answer to the question makes it very clear if you should be engaging in that activity, or if your time could be spent more productively elsewhere.

Once you begin looking at your daily activities through the filter of your goals, you will see some remarkable changes in the way you live your life. You'll live each day in a much more focused, productive, and satisfying way. When you know what you want to accomplish in life, you will no longer tolerate those time bleeding, energy draining activities that nibble away at your life and keep you from your goals.

You'll turn off the TV, watch fewer movies, waste less time scrolling through your phone, and become more selective in how you spend social time and with who. As a result, you'll devote more of your life to the things that matter—and you'll see a marked acceleration toward your objectives in life.

You may have asked yourself, "What is my sense of mission, purpose and calling?" Many ask, but few pray and think it through until they get an answer. Having a *life goal* is not the end; it is the beginning of a lifetime of adventure with God. Your life goal is the target at which you aim the arrow of your life. It is the destination you choose to reach. Along the way there will be detours, roadblocks, and naysayers. That is part of the great adventure! Don't miss it because of fear or because you gave up too soon.

When setting life goals, think big! Don't place limits on your goals and dreams.

What if your goal is so big that it intimidates you?

What if your dream is so vast that you don't even know where to begin? No problem! You simply break down your big life goal into a series of more bite size goals that keep you moving forward.

If Shamgar had known from the outset that it was going to be one Hebrew farmer versus 600 Philistines, he probably would have thrown up his hands and said,

THE POWER OF ONE

"Why even start? It's hopeless! It's humanly impossible!" The reason Shamgar was able to do what he did was that he broke his big goal ("I will save my nation") down into a series of smaller goals ("I will defeat these twelve or twenty Philistines"). And he even broke those smaller goals down into even smaller goals ("I will skewer this big bruiser, then the next one, and the one after that").

You and I should approach goal setting the same way. You can accomplish any "extreme dream" if you break it down into doable chunks. A marathon seems like a daunting challenge until you look at it as a series of twenty-six, one-mile goals. Writing a book seems intimidating—until you realize that it's just a matter of persistently writing one chapter after another. Losing fifty pounds seems like an impossible task until we realize that it's just a matter of losing a pound a week for a year with a sensible diet and exercise plan.

The late Rich DeVos, my friend and boss, the original owner of the Orlando Magic and founder of the Amway Corporation, started by bottling his products in his own basement and selling them himself. By the time he retired, he had built his company into a seven-billion-dollar global operation. He was once asked how he and his partner did it. "All Jay and I ever did," he said, "was get up every day and go to work, and add another distributor, another product, another country."

The way to achieve big goals is to break them down into little goals. Every step you make along the way enables you to mark your progress toward your "extreme dream." Long-term goals look five to ten years into the future. They are clear, measurable goals with a long but definite deadline: "I will complete my novel within five years from this date," or "I will move to Nepal and open a youth hostel by the end of this decade." Goals should never be fuzzy or vague; goal setting should never be confused with "wishing and hoping." When you set a long-range goal, you should know exactly what you want to accomplish, when you expect to accomplish it and how you plan to get it done.

You should break your long-term goals down into mid-range goals that look a year or two into the future. Mid-range goals are intermediate steps that help advance you toward your long-range goals. Mid-range goals should be divided into short-range goals consisting of the various tasks you have to carry out over the next few weeks to move you along to your mid-range goals. And, of course, your short-range goals should be broken down into daily "Things to Do" lists.

What should your goals be? No one can decide that but you. It's not easy to set goals, but it's essential if you want to successfully complete your mission in life. A person with a clear set of goals can achieve practically anything in life. A person without goals is going nowhere.

THE POWER OF ONE

Your long-range and life goals should be BIG. Don't be timid when you are setting goals for your life. Sam Walton, the founder of Walmart, said, "I believe in always having goals and setting them high." And media magnate Ted Turner observed, "My father always said, 'Never set goals you can reach in your lifetime, because there's nothing left after you accomplish them.'"

Goals should be written down, not just remembered. Written goals are visible, tangible, and memorable. When you write down your goals, you can post them on your refrigerator or set them as digital wallpaper. You want to keep them in front of you as a constant reminder. Writing down your goals is a good way of programming them into your conscious and subconscious mind.

When you set goals, set a deadline. A goal without a deadline is just a fantasy. Deadlines force you to focus on your goals in a persistent and concrete way. When you know you have a deadline to achieve your goals, you tend to get up earlier, work harder and stay later to get your tasks done. Deadlines force you to prioritize and organize more effectively.

Florence Chadwick was a world-class swimmer who set a record in 1950 by swimming the English Channel (from France to England) in thirteen hours and twenty minutes—a distance of twenty-one miles at the Dover Straits. In 1951, she swam the Channel from England to France, becoming the first woman in history to achieve this feat from both shores. In 1952, Florence Chadwick set out to conquer an even longer distance, the twenty-six miles between Catalina Island and the California shore at Palos Verdes. The water was icy, and shark infested, but she wasn't worried about the fins that circled around her. There was only one thing that worried Florence Chadwick: a blanket of gray fog.

She set out from Catalina and made good time during the first twelve hours of the swim. But then the fog closed in. After fifteen hours, unable to see the coastline, Chadwick conceded defeat and climbed into the escort boat. She later admitted that she simply lost her desire to press on. "It was the fog," she said. "If I could have seen land, I could have finished. But when you can't see your goal, you lose all sense of progress, and you begin to give up."

How far was Florence Chadwick when she gave up on her quest? A mere one-half mile. She had covered *98 percent of the* distance to her objective and gave up with *only 2 percent* of the distance remaining!

A few months later, she repeated the attempt—and she reached her goal in thirteen hours and forty-seven minutes, breaking a record set in 1927 by a male swimmer. Why was she able to reach her goal on the second attempt? Because the sun was shining, and it was easy for Chadwick to keep her objective in view.

The same is true for you and me. We need to set specific goals, write them down and keep them always before us. Setting goals is a crucial part of starting where you are, using what you have and doing what you can.

Work Hard

It may seem like stating the obvious, but nothing of importance is ever accomplished without hard work. The hardest part of hard work is getting started. For writers, the hardest task of all is sitting down at the keyboard and typing that first sentence. For musicians, the hardest part about practicing is opening the instrument case. As J. R. R. Tolkien, author of *The Lord of the Rings* trilogy, once said, "It's a job that's never started that takes the longest to finish." The essential factor that separates successes from failures is the willingness and discipline to work hard.

Olympia J. Snowe, United States Senator from Maine, acquired her strong work ethic from her aunt. She recalls, "My aunt used to say to me, 'Olympia, don't ever wait for me to ask you. Look around and see if there's something that needs to be done and do it.' So, guess what? Now, I can't sit still! As soon as I sit down, I find myself thinking, 'What needs to be done?' and I start doing it. I can't help myself."

I tell my children all the time that the two most important words in the English language are "What else?" As in, "What else can I do? What else can I offer? What else can I contribute?" If you are a "what else?"

person, you will always be in demand, because there aren't very many of them out there.

Kemmons Wilson was nine months old when his father died. "I never knew him," Wilson recalled. "Early on, I was so hungry when I was growing up that I was scared that I might be hungry again. I became a hard worker. I enjoy working." Born in 1913, Wilson was fourteen and making drugstore deliveries on his bicycle when he was hit by a car and nearly killed. His injuries kept him laid up for a year, and doctors said he would never walk again. Wilson proved the doctors wrong.

In 1951, Kemmons Wilson was vacationing with his family, and he became incensed over the high price and poor quality of family motels. He decided to start his own chain of motels and called it Holiday Inn. He set high quality standards, air-conditioned every room, and offered a pool and restaurant at every location. In the process, he revolutionized the hospitality industry.

Wilson once wrote a pamphlet called *Twenty Tips for Success.* The first of those twenty tips: "Work only a half a day; it makes no difference which half—it can be either the first twelve hours or the last twelve hours." Wilson followed his own advice. Until shortly before his death at age ninety, Kemmons Wilson continued to put in twelve-hour workdays.

Legendary ad man David Ogilvy, founder of Ogilvy and Mather, said, "I admire people who work with gusto. If you don't enjoy what you are doing, I beg

THE POWER OF ONE

you to find another job. Remember the Scottish proverb: 'Be happy while you're living, for you're a long time dead.'"

Some people say that the ability to work hard can compensate for a lack of talent—to which the late, great British prime minister, Winston Churchill, replied, "The ability to work hard is, in itself, a talent." If you can work hard—and I mean ten, twelve, fourteen or more hours a day—then you will set yourself far apart from the great mass of humanity. You will distinguish yourself and you will earn great rewards. Why? Because, to put it bluntly, most people are lazy. Everyone wants to enjoy the lifestyle of the rich and famous, but few are willing to put in the hard work and sacrifice required to attain it. As Zig Ziglar once said, "There is no traffic jam on the extra mile."

Doak Walker was a four-time All-Pro halfback who led the Detroit Lions to two NFL titles. He once said, "No champion has ever achieved his goal without showing more dedication than the next person; working harder than the next person; making more sacrifices than the next person; training and conditioning himself more than the next person; studying harder than the next person; enjoying his final goal more than the next person."

Those who put out a 100 percent effort never have cause (or time!) for regrets. The person who puts out a 98 percent effort sometimes does. George Plimpton, in his book *The X Factor: A Quest for Excellence,* tells the story of Willie Davis, star defensive end for the Green Bay Packers in the 1960s. Today, Davis is a successful businessman, a radio industry CEO, and a director on the boards of such companies as Dow Chemical, MGM, and Sara Lee. Despite all his success, both in and out of football, he has one major regret that haunts him to this day.

Davis was playing in a game against the Philadelphia Eagles. Late in the game, he saw an Eagles ballcarrier streaking down the far sideline. Davis knew he had the speed to reach him—but why bother? There were other Packer's defenders who were in position to catch him. Why, Davis wondered, should he wear himself out when his teammates would surely bring the ballcarrier down? Davis dogged it and let the runner go.

The Eagles ballcarrier slipped the Packers' tacklers and scored a touchdown. In the end, that score cost the Packers the game. As he went to the locker room, all Willie Davis could think of was the fact that he had a chance to prevent that touchdown, but he let the runner go—just because he didn't want to work too hard. He had made a conscious decision not to put out the extra effort would have won the game. He knew he would live with that regret for the rest of his life.

That day, Willie Davis made a life changing decision. As he told George Plimpton, "Never again would I come out of any situation wondering if I could

THE POWER OF ONE

have done a job better. That principle is as important to me today as it was then. Every day, I tell myself not to let an opportunity slide by that I could have taken advantage of."

We like to pretend that we are working at 100 percent of capacity every day—and that on those rare occasions when we stay a half hour after work or do a little work over the weekend, we are giving 110 percent. That was the attitude of a young Bill Walton when he was playing basketball for Coach John Wooden at UCLA. When Wooden told Walton that he needed to put out more effort, Walton said, "Coach, I'm already putting out 110 percent!" To this, Coach Wooden replied, "No one can give 110 percent! Don't you know anything about mathematics?"

It's true. Most of us get by with an effort that is closer to 50 or 60 percent of our capacity. If we manage to work up a little sweat, we think we are giving 110 percent, but we're only at 70 or 80 percent. If we ever truly gave a 100 percent effort to reaching an important goal, we would find out that we can achieve far more than we ever dreamed possible.

If you can discipline yourself to work hard, you can achieve just about any goal you set your mind to. If you feel that hard work is just too much of an imposition on your cushy lifestyle, then you must accept the fact that you will never rise above the level of mediocrity. To be a successful person, you must work very hard at doing what you can.

Compete Intensely

You've got to love Shamgar's competitive spirit! He took on 600 heavily armored Philistines—and he beat them! People who make a real difference in the world are invariably people who are competitive.

Understand, a competitive person isn't merely someone who wants to win. A competitor wants to be the best. That's why people who cheat to win are not true competitors. They're frauds. True competitors don't compete to pump up their own egos or reputations. They compete to raise the level of their own performance.

To be a true competitor, you must love and respect your opponent. Why? Because your opponent forces you to elevate your performance and be the best you can be. Sure, winning is important—but excellence is even more important. The late Wayne Calloway, who was chairman and CEO of PepsiCo from 1986 to 1996, said, "Nothing focuses the mind better than the constant sight of a competitor who wants to wipe you off the map."

Pat Summitt, women's basketball coach at the University of Tennessee and a six-time NCAA Championship winner, put it this way: "Your competitors make you better. Having worthy adversaries stimulate your work ethic and brings out qualities you may not have known you had. Don't resent them. You

THE POWER OF ONE

should love your competitors and thank them. Competitiveness is what separates achievers from the average. Only by learning to compete can you discover just how much you can achieve. Trust me, you have more within you than you realize. Competition is one of the great tools for exploring yourself and surprising yourself."

Paula Newby-Fraser is an eight-time Ironman Triathlon World Champion and has been acclaimed by ABC's Wide World of Sports as "The Greatest All-Around Female Athlete in the World." She said, "When you compete against someone of equal or greater ability, it can lift your energy and mental concentration to new heights. A certain degree of positive stress can be very beneficial and can motivate you to work harder. The key is to see your rivalry as your guiding light, as a tool you can use to find the potential within yourself. Instead of wishing a competitor ill fortune, the healthy athlete wants a rival to succeed so they both can rise to a whole new level."

Authentic competition is honest competition. Entrepreneur William Simon, who once ran for governor of California, said, "The whole point of free enterprise, of capitalism, is vigorous, honest competition. Every corner cut, every bribe placed, every little cheating move by a businessman in pursuit of quick plunder instead of honest profit, is an outright attack on the real free enterprise system."

In recent years, the advocates of so-called political correctness have tried to rid our society of competition, claiming that there is something fundamentally unfair about any system that produces winners and losers. After all, losing makes people feel bad! (And after all these years in the pro sports business, don't I know it!)

But the truth is that, try as we might, we can't root competitiveness out of the human spirit—nor should we want to. Competition is good for the soul. It's good for business, for sports, for education, for every human endeavor. Competition raises standards and produces excellence. Competition is here to stay.

In his book *Who Needs God*, Rabbi Harold Kushner (author of *When Bad Things Happen to Good People*) tells the story of a young premed sophomore at Stanford. As a reward for his excellent grades in school, his parents gave him an expense-paid vacation to the Far East. While in Asia, the young man met a guru who said, "By seeking after success, young man, you are destroying your soul. You study and study to get a better grade than your friend. Your idea of a happy marriage is to marry the prettiest girl in school, the girl all your friends want. You are constantly competing with those around you. People were not meant to live that way. Give up your striving. Join us here in the ashram, where there is no striving, no competition—only meditation, sharing and joy."

The young man found the guru's message persuasive, so he joined the ashram. He phoned his parents and told them about his decision. His parents were heartbroken. They urged their son to come back home and pursue a career in medicine, but he was adamant. "Sorry. I don't want all that striving and competition. I just want to live in the ashram and experience true peace and bliss."

Six months passed. Finally, the young man's parents received a letter from their son in the Far East. "Dear Mom and Dad," it read. "I know you weren't pleased with the decision I made, but I want you to know how happy I've been here in the ashram. For the first time in my life, I've found peace. Here there is no striving, no competition, no one trying to beat out the next guy. We all share everything equally, and my soul is experiencing true harmony and joy at last." He signed the letter, then added a P.S.: "One more thing—I've only been here six months and I'm already the number two disciple in the ashram! If I keep working at my meditating, I think I can be number one by June!"

You can't get away from competition! And you shouldn't want to. Competition is about being your best. The competitiveness of Shamgar enabled him to beat six-hundred-to-one odds. A competitive spirit will enable you to swing the odds in your favor, too.

Persevere

Perseverance is more important than brains, skill, talent, or luck. One of my most memorable lessons in the importance of perseverance came during the summer following the eighth grade. I tried out for a semipro baseball team, and though all the other players were much older, I made the team. Even so, I was worried about whether I could really perform at the same level as the other players.

On the way to my first game, I rode in the backseat while my mother drove. My grandmother sat up front next to Mom. As we drove, we talked about my prospects with the team. "Well," I said at one point, "if it doesn't work out, I can always quit."

With a suddenness that startled me, my grandmother whirled around, jabbed one finger in my chest and said, "You don't quit! Nobody in this family quits!" I got the message. And I didn't quit.

I am a father to nineteen children—four by birth, fourteen by international adoption (Romania, South Korea, the Philippines, and Brazil), and one by remarriage. Because of my large family, people ask me all the time, "Are there any common traits you notice among all of your kids?" And yes, there is one trait I've seen in all my kids at one time or another: Whenever things get tough, they say, "I know how to fix that—I'll quit!"

It doesn't matter whether it's the swimming team or advanced math or an after-school job stacking boxes—when the going gets tough, most kids want to quit. They want easy paths, smooth as glass. One of my

THE POWER OF ONE

most important missions as a father is to turn young quitters into persistent winners by convincing them that quitting is a permanent solution to a temporary problem.

I love to read—especially biographies of great people. I've read a ton of them, and I've discovered a common thread in the lives of all influential men and women: No matter what culture or period of history they lived in, they all had extraordinary obstacles to overcome; they all suffered setbacks, heartaches, and defeats; and they all refused to quit. Read the life story of any great individual—Abraham Lincoln, Eleanor Roosevelt, Winston Churchill, Martin Luther King, Jr., Walt Disney, Frederick Douglass, Helen Keller, Galileo, Louis Pasteur, Ludwig van Beethoven, Jackie Robinson, Gandhi, Rosa Parks—and you will see a person who possessed an inner intensity that refused to quit. These individuals would climb over, scramble around, tunnel under or simply dynamite any obstacle in their way. If at any point they had said, "I quit," we would never have heard of them.

As I write these words, I have run thirty-one marathons. A marathon, of course, is a cross-country footrace that is 26.2 miles from start to finish. It is one of the most punishing things you can do to the human body. People ask me, "Why do you put yourself through that kind of torture?" My answer: Running marathons is the best way I know to practice perseverance.

After the first eight or ten miles of a marathon, my body and head are screaming, "Stop this foolishness! Give it up! End this pain! Quit, quit, quit!" But unless you have run a marathon, you can't imagine the euphoric feeling of crossing that finish line. When you've run a marathon, my friend, you know that you can persevere!

Many years ago, an ambitious young employee of the Ford Motor Company sought out the boss himself, Henry Ford, and asked, "Mr. Ford, how can I be successful in life?"

Without hesitating, Ford answered, "When you start something, finish it."

Henry Ford knew the power of perseverance. He went broke five times before he finally succeeded in the automobile business. Though his successes were great, his failures were embarrassing. The very first Ford Motor car had a glaring design defect: Ford forgot to install a reverse gear! But he knew how to achieve his goals—never give up. Never quit.

After a concert, a woman once came up to violin virtuoso Fritz Kreisler and said, "Oh, Mr. Kreisler, I'd give my life to play as beautifully as you!" "Madam," Kreisler answered, "I have." To be a virtuoso at the violin or at anything else, you must persevere. Never give up, never quit.

Tom Monahan bought a struggling hole-in-the-wall pizza shop in 1960. The shop continued to struggle under his ownership for eight years—then he lost the entire

THE POWER OF ONE

business in a fire. The insurance company paid him ten cents on the dollar. He took the money, invested in a new pizza shop, and after two years fell behind in his loan payments and lost the shop to the bank.

In 1971, with debts of over $1.5 million, with his creditors threatening lawsuits, Monahan asked himself, "How can I turn this around?" The answer that came to him: home delivery. People could pick up the phone, call his shop and he would have the pizza delivered to the customer's home within thirty minutes.

Though we take pizza delivery for granted today, no one ever offered home-delivered pizza before Tom Monahan invented the concept. Today, his company—Domino's Pizza—has more than 20,000 corporate and franchise stores in more than fifty countries and is still adding more. Tom Monahan is living proof that the key to success is perseverance—never give up. Don't quit.

Today, Michael Blake is a successful novelist and screenwriter. But for most of his life, he felt like a failure. He had left home at age seventeen, wrote more than twenty screenplays plus several novels and received nothing but rejections for twenty-five years. Still, he refused to give up.

At age forty-two, he finally made his first sale—a novel called *Dances with Wolves*. He had spent months working on it while living out of his car and washing dishes in a Chinese restaurant in Arizona. When he completed the manuscript, he dedicated it to his friends

Viggo Mortensen and Exene Cervenka, with whom he had been staying for several weeks.

Actor-producer Kevin Costner bought the rights to the novel and hired Blake to write the screenplay. Costner's film of *Dances with Wolves* won the Academy Award as best picture. After years of failure and rejection, Michael Blake was finally on his way.

"Successful people," said motivational author Napoleon Hill, "usually find that great success lies just beyond the point when they're convinced that their idea is not going to work."

And legendary boxer James "Gentleman Jim" Corbett, who KO'd the great John L. Sullivan in a grueling twenty-one-round fight in New Orleans in 1892, put it this way:

Fight one more round when your feet are so tired that you have to shuffle back to the center of the ring—fight one more round.

When your arms are so tired you can hardly lift your hands to come on guard—fight one more round.

When your nose is bleeding, and your eyes are black, and you are so tired you wish your opponent would crack you on the jaw and put you to sleep—fight one more round.

Remembering that the man who always fights one more round is never whipped.

An ancient proverb from China puts it even more succinctly: "Fall down seven times; get up eight."

THE POWER OF ONE

There is one quality that is common to all successful people, all people who have ever made a difference in this world: persistence.

They started where they were, they used what they had, they did what they could. They never surrendered. They held on and held out. They refused to quit.

Serve Others

We have all been placed on this earth for a reason. And our reason for living has nothing to do with being rich or famous or successful. It has nothing to do with what we gain. It has everything to do with what we give. It has to do with the things we say and do and sacrifice to serve others.

Nobel Prize Winner, Mother Teresa, spent her life among the impoverished and diseased. She never owned land or a home and was not educated beyond the training for nuns in Dublin. As a 12-year-old girl in Macedonia, she felt that God was calling her to devote her life completely to him. She left home at the age of eighteen and joined a community of nuns. After training in Dublin, she went to India in where she took her vows, taught in Calcutta, and began to feel that God was calling her to a ministry beyond those convent walls.

Some years later she obtained permission to leave the convent school and devote herself to working in the slums of Calcutta. She started an open-air school for the children of the slums and two years later opened

Missionaries of Charity, to serve the needs of people who had been forgotten by society. In those early days, the outreach of the Missionaries of Charity was primarily to people with leprosy, who were dying alone and friendless in the streets of Calcutta. Today, the Missionaries of Charity has a global ministry, helping the poorest of the poor, victims of natural catastrophes, homeless people, shut-ins, alcoholics, and AIDS sufferers. Mother Teresa started where she was – a 12-year-old with a strong call from God; used what she had – no funds, but a heart that yearned with compassion for the suffering; did what she could - she depended on Divine Providence and started an open-air school for slum children. Financial backing and volunteers caught the vision and came alongside for the mission. [20]

Often, when Mother Teresa traveled to speak in Europe and America, her listeners would be moved with a desire to do something, anything, to help the poor and suffering people of Calcutta. They would come to her after her talk, or they would write letters, saying, "I want to help the poor and the lepers. Please tell me how I can join you and work with you in Calcutta."

She knew that people sometimes got caught up in the emotion of the moment when they heard the heart-tugging story of some poor leper or an orphaned child on the streets in India. She knew that some people had romanticized notions of going to an exotic city and finding meaning in their lives by ministering to needy

THE POWER OF ONE

people. She knew that emotionalism and romanticism were the wrong reasons for wanting to serve others. She often replied: "Stay where you are. Find your own Calcutta. Find the sick, the suffering and the lonely right there where you are—in your own homes and in your own families, in your workplaces and in your schools. You can find Calcutta all over the world if you have the eyes to see. Everywhere, wherever you go, you find people who are unwanted, unloved, uncared for, rejected by society—completely forgotten.

And she was right. Calcutta is all around us—if we have the eyes to see. It may not feel as grand a gesture or adventure to serve the needy people we find right in our own neighborhoods. We think of sacrificing in Calcutta more worthy than for the needy in central Los Angeles or the south side of Chicago, or in the any of the inner city streets that fill America. The need is all around us, and the need is great.

Voltaire wrote, "Every man is guilty of all the good he did not do."[22] We have received so many blessings from God that are beyond our ability to deserve or repay, and "Service to others," as the great Muhammad Ali once said, "is the rent you pay for your room here on earth."[23]

But what should we do? How should we serve other people? By now, you shouldn't even have to ask such a question. If you have money, give money. If you have time, give time. If you have love, give love. When showing love to others, begin by serving the people you don't like. Jesus put it this way: "Love your enemies, do good to them, and lend to them without expecting to get anything back. Then your reward will be great, and you will be sons of the Most High, because he is kind to the ungrateful and wicked" (Luke 6:35).

In *Mere Christianity*, C. S. Lewis wrote, "Do not waste time bothering whether you 'love' your neighbor; act as if you did. As soon as we do this, we find one of the great secrets. When you are behaving as if you loved someone, you will presently come to love him. If you injure someone you dislike, you will find yourself disliking him more. If you do him a good turn, you will find yourself disliking him less."[21]

A life of serving others does not mean that we must impoverish ourselves or that we cannot be successful in terms of our finances and our careers. John Wesley, the godly founder of the Methodist church, was deeply involved in ministering to the poor and the outcasts of his society. In a 1760 sermon called "The Use of Money," he said, "Gain all you can, save all you can, give all you can. Do all the good you can, in all the ways you can, to all the souls you can, in every place you can, at all times you can, with all the zeal you can, as long as you can."[8]

John Wesley was saying to us in words the same thing Shamgar says to us through his actions: Start where you are, use what you have, do what you can.

THE POWER OF ONE

When John Alexander was president of InterVarsity Christian Fellowship, he used to ask students a penetrating question: "What have you done this past year to make a helpful difference within one mile of your home?"

Ouch! That is a painful question, isn't it?

The truth is that there are hurting, suffering, friendless, hopeless, needy souls within a mile of your doorstep, within walking distance, perhaps right next door to you. You don't have to go to Calcutta. Find your own Calcutta. Find someone to serve. Find someone to love. Find someone to save. St. Francis of Assisi once said, "Start by doing what is necessary. Then do what is possible. Suddenly, you are doing the impossible."

What can you do, right where you are? And how soon can you do it?

SEVEN

Cancel the Noise

– Jay Strack

Don't let the noise of others' opinions drown out your own inner voice." Steve Jobs

I challenge you to dare to focus on canceling the noise around you. You will then become a creative explorer, planner, and doer beyond what you ever expected. More significant adventures than you can imagine will come to you when you open up to new relationships, listen intentionally, and serve others without condition.

    A friend called one day and invited me to an auction at Sotheby's in New York. He had taken me to Sotheby's in London, where I met Eric Clapton and shared a sentence of my salvation story, so I was anxious to see who would surprise me this time. A lovely woman was introduced to me as Mrs. Coretta Scott King. My first thought was to bow before royalty, but she smiled and warmly greeted me. How in the world did I get this privilege? The family of the slain civil rights leader, Dr. Martin Luther King, Jr., walked us through some of Dr. King's archives, and I was fascinated by every inch. When we reached one particular case, one of the family members chuckled and said, "Take a look." Dr. King's "Transcript of Record" from Crozer Theological Seminary was inside. This report showed his lowest grade, a "C," in public speaking.[24]

As one of the family told me that day, the professor did not believe Martin's flamboyant speaking style would be effective. We enjoyed a good laugh over that, given his legacy as one of the great public speakers of our time and author of perhaps the most repeated speech in history, "I Have a Dream." I wonder if the professor was watching the speech of his former student televised across America on August 28, 1963, as he stood on the steps of the Lincoln Memorial. His voice rolled with intensity across the vast crowd of people of many races with a message that is still unforgettable decades later. Martin Luther King canceled the noise of his professor and all the critics of his movement to bring peace to our nation. And we are all glad he did.

I have a dream that my four children will one day live in a nation where they will not be judged by the color of their skin but by the content of their character. I have a dream that one day every valley shall be exalted, every hill and mountain shall be made low, the rough places will be made plain, and the crooked places will be made straight, and the glory of the Lord shall be revealed, and all flesh shall see it together. This will be the day when all of God's children will be able to sing with a new

THE POWER OF ONE

meaning, "My country 'tis of thee, sweet land of liberty, of thee I sing. Land where my fathers died, land of the pilgrim's pride, from every mountainside, let freedom ring." When we let freedom ring, when we let it ring from every village and every hamlet, from every state and every city, we will be able to speed up that day when all of God's children, black men and white men, Jews and Gentiles, Protestants and Catholics, will be able to join hands and sing in the words of the old Negro spiritual, "Free at last! Free at last! Thank God Almighty, we are free at last!"

The world has profoundly benefited from Dr. King's words that continue to lift hearts and fill us with a vision for a world beyond hatred, injustice, and racial division. Because he rejected discouragement, his great words are burned into our history books for all generations to come.

I am sure that Shamgar heard the same type of well-intentioned but misguided advice in his day. I know I have. Perhaps Shamgar's neighbors and family said, "Don't be a fool! You can't take on Philistine army by yourself! You don't have armor or a decent spear or sword! You're crazy to even try! It won't work!"

Given the odds against him, this sounds like logical advice. It stands to reason that one warrior against 600 will lose. If the Philistines captured him, torture was more than possible. But Shamgar knew he had to do what he could, even if it cost him his life. Win or lose, he would remain faithful to God and his nation.

A Chinese proverb states, "The person who says it cannot be done should not interrupt the person doing it." Cleaning up the R-rated version of General Patton, I labeled the theme of our early SLU days as "Lead, follow, or get out of the way." My father served under WWII's infamous General of the 2nd Armored Division, nicknamed "Hell on Wheels." Patton meant it, and we won many battles because he did.

With the best intentions, people will tell you, "Don't waste your time writing that book. Don't waste your money starting a business right now. Don't waste your compassion on those people. Don't waste your life serving others when you could use your talent to become rich and influential. Don't worry about your grades; just have fun at college." Most of the bad advice you'll receive in life comes with a side order of good intentions. But what value are good intentions if they only serve to keep you from your goals?

"Bully advice" is when people insist you listen and act on their thoughts. Thank them for their concern but ask God to show you truth and hope. Prayer may lead you to change plans or directions, but always continue dreaming. There is always a way to serve while you wait. I have discovered a season of waiting can evolve into rich days of discovery and intimacy with the Savior.

THE POWER OF ONE

Exodus 14 is one of my favorite passages to preach. The children of Israel were standing at the foot of the Red Sea with the enemy hot on their tail. It was impossible, it seemed, to go forward, and many began to say, "Let's just go back! Let us give ourselves back to the Egyptians as slaves, and perhaps they will let us live. Didn't we tell you we should have stayed?" Liar, liar, pants on fire for sure. No one ever said, "Let's stay here and be slaves." But when the odds became too big, they began to give in to the past instead of thinking about what could be in the future.

"Moses answered the people, "Do not be afraid. Stand firm and you will see the deliverance the Lord will bring you today. The Egyptians you see today you will never see again. The Lord will fight for you; you need only to be still" Exodus 14:13-14

Moses was looking for a compromise when he declared, "Stand firm!" Again, it sounds like good intentions. But the Lord rebuked Moses for his lack of creative thinking. In verse 15, we hear the roar of God to "*Move on!*"

"Then the Lord said to Moses, "Why are you crying out to me? Tell the Israelites to move on. Raise your staff and stretch out your hand over the sea to divide the water so that the Israelites can go through the sea on dry ground. Exodus 14:15-16

Going against the odds may not have a visible win at first glance, but when you think deeply about what could be, you can step forward and *"Move on."*

You Are Chosen

Some of the worst advice you'll ever receive comes from inside you. It manifests in the form of self-doubt, self-criticism, and self-accusation. In Exodus 4:10 when God chose Moses to deliver the people of Israel from slavery in Egypt, Moses protested: *"Pardon your servant, Lord. I have never been eloquent, neither in the past nor since you have spoken to your servant. I am slow of speech and tongue."* Some scholars believe that the phrase "slow of speech and tongue refers to a speech impediment—perhaps a problem with stuttering. Moses hesitated because he felt overwhelmed.

God replied, *"Who gave human beings their mouths? Who makes them deaf or mute? Who gives them sight or makes them blind? Is it not I, the Lord? Now go; I will help you speak and will teach you what to say."* (Ex 4:11-12)

In other words, don't focus on what you can't do. Instead, focus on the One who has the power to enable you to do anything. Your job is to decide to move forward; God will give you the power to speak and to finish well.

THE POWER OF ONE

Like Moses, we are easily overwhelmed by what we can't do instead of simply doing what we can. When God gives us a task or a mission to complete, we look at our resources and say, "No way! I'm not up to this! I could never do anything like this!" Author Helen Keller was blind and deaf. She once wrote, "The only thing worse than being blind is to have sight with no vision." We find ourselves in that situation when we stop and stand still because we cannot immediately or physically see the win.

God sees the big picture, even when we can't. He says to us the same thing He said, in effect, to Moses: "You think you can't do this; but with My power working in you, you can do anything. You just do what you can, and I'll do the rest. Don't be so focused on what you can't do that you fail to do what you can, and it will be enough. I will not ask you to do more than you can handle."

Sometimes, we feel as insignificant as a single grain of sand on the beach. We think, "I'm just one little person. I don't have much to offer God in the way of talent or resources." I have been in rooms with high political officials, sports celebrities, and many heroes of the faith. My thoughts were, "What are you doing here, Jay? You don't belong in this group." In those moments, I think of the stories of E. V. Hill, Martin Luther King, and Shamgar, and I become confident that God has placed me there. Instead of talking, I listen. I ask how to help and look for ways to serve. And 100% of the time, I have been able to share Jesus, maybe not with a Bible, but through servant leadership in the name of Jesus.

Many have displayed teaching examples of servant leadership for me. One of the stickiest memories is the first time I met Tony Dungy. I was invited to speak at a chapel for the Tampa Bay Bucs and arrived early to be sure I was in the right place, so I wasn't surprised to find only one person in the room. He was organizing chairs for the morning's meeting. I said, "Excuse me, sir, do you know if this is where the Bucs are holding their chapel this morning?" He said, "This is it." I put out my hand to introduce myself – "My name is Jay. Do you need any help setting up these chairs?" He replied, "Thank you, but I am fine. My name is Tony." I smiled and went down to the hall to wait. Suddenly, it hit me – Tony is the name of the new coach of the Bucs! Why would they have the coach set up chairs? I returned to the room and asked, "Can I help you set up?" "No, thank you. I like to pray over each chair before the chapel. All these young men will face a hundred battles that are not on the field." It is no wonder Coach Dungy went on to win a Super Bowl and be an inductee into the Pro Football Hall of Fame. I have never forgotten the impact of those moments.

One of my favorite books is *The Five Practices of Exemplary Leadership* by authors Kouzes and Posner.

THE POWER OF ONE

On my desk is my handwritten quote: "Exemplary leaders are forward looking and able to gaze across the horizon of time as they imagine greater opportunities to come." At the edge of the battle, in our feelings of powerlessness and insignificance, the secrets of Shamgar empower us to move forward. God doesn't call us to be talented, powerful, or wealthy. He calls us to start where we are, use what we have, and do what we can.

By simply doing what we can, as Shamgar did, we may be able to save a soul, a life, a neighborhood, a cause, or a nation. You never know. And the best news is that we don't have to worry about the results because the results are God's business. Our part is to do what we can.

You may think, "But it's too late for me. I've been on the sidelines too long. I'm too old to get in the game. I am happy to sit here and be God's benchwarmer." As I am researching stories for this book, a TV news report flashed on the screen about a 95-year-old Holocaust survivor and former IDF soldier walking into the Israeli troops to rally them with a dance and speech. My first thought was, "What can I do to rally the troops?" And what can you do to rally the troops? It's only too late if you choose it to be.

We don't know how old Shamgar was when he heard God's call, but he may have been prodding the oxen for quite a while, waiting for his chance to get in the game. After all those years pushing a plow and looking at the south end of a northbound ox, did Shamgar have what it takes to launch a guerilla campaign against the Philistines?

Shamgar didn't know. There was no way he could. He had never done anything like that before. Shamgar knew only one thing for sure: win, lose, or draw, he had to do what he could. What about Shamgar's lack of training in the art of war? How could a farm boy do a soldier's job?

A few years ago, I came across an article that said duct tape is useless for ductwork. Once I started researching the idea, I found many articles that agreed. "Duct tape helps repair just about anything, but ironically, not ducts."[25]

What's the point? People and duct tape will surprise you. They often perform better at tasks they were not meant for than those they should logically excel in. A woman with a degree in art history could run a dot-com business. A man with an MBA in business could end up in the pulpit or running a nonprofit. To the surprise of all who knew him, a farmer named Shamgar became a military genius, national hero, and judge of Israel. You never know. People and duct tape are full of surprises.

You may think you were born to be a farmer, a salesperson, a banker, a stockbroker, a computer programmer, a teacher, a vocalist, or an actor—but God may have a better idea! You might discover He has a

THE POWER OF ONE

plan and a purpose for your life that you never imagined. You may find yourself accomplishing things you never dreamed you could do. It may not be what you planned to do with your life; it may not be what you trained for in college, but it just may be God's plan and purpose.

And if God created you to do it, you will love it! God's task or mission for your life will fit you like a glove.

Low-Intensity Winning

Shamgar, you may recall, was the third judge in Israel. The first two judges, Othniel and Ehud, were military men who won great military battles. Othniel went to war and won a significant battle over the army of the king of Aram. As a result of Othniel's victory, the land of Israel was at peace for forty years. The second judge in Israel was Ehud, a brilliant strategist who personally carried out an assassination plot against the evil King Eglon of Moab. Then Ehud led the army of Israel into battle against the army of Moab, killing ten thousand enemy soldiers in a single day. Not one Moabite soldier escaped. The land of Israel experienced eighty years of peace after Ehud's victory.

Judges 3:31 gives Shamgar an honorable mention: *"After Ehud came Shamgar son of Anath, who struck down 600 Philistines with an ox goad. He, too, saved Israel."* The writer of Judges mentions Shamgar almost as a footnote or an "Oh, by the way" sort of remark. Shamgar didn't conquer the nation of Aram or the nation of Moab. He didn't lead an attack that slaughtered ten thousand men in a single day. Shamgar engaged in what the Pentagon calls "low-intensity conflict" or guerilla warfare. The Pentagon has other names such as "insurgency," "special warfare," or "limited politico-military struggle." That type of warfare may only get a part of the chapter in the history books, but it is valuable, nevertheless. Usually, as in Shamgar's case, low-intensity conflict only rates a footnote. Shamgar was a guerilla fighter. And guerilla fighters never get the glory that Five-Star generals get.

We don't know for sure who wrote the book of Judges, though some Bible scholars think it was probably the prophet Samuel. No one would blame Shamgar for being miffed at his biographer. After all, Shamgar saved Israel, just as Othniel and Ehud did—and he did it alone, armed only with an ox goad! Isn't that worth at least one whole chapter of narrative? But no! Shamgar gets merely two scattered verses.

Unlike Othniel and Ehud, Shamgar didn't win a big, spectacular battle. We don't know how long it took Shamgar to rack up 600 notches on his ox goad, but it almost certainly didn't happen in a single day. He likely won a few skirmishes at a time, spread over weeks or months, if not years.

Open any book about WWII, and you will find detailed accounts of the most famous battles—Anzio and

THE POWER OF ONE

Monte Cassino, the London Blitz, the Battle of the Bulge, D-Day, Leyte Gulf, Midway, Guadalcanal, Iwo Jima, and on and on. But what about the lesser-known battles that also helped decide the war? The victories of the Filipino guerillas over the Japanese at Balete Pass and Ipo Dam? Or the almost forgotten battles of the Free French guerillas against the Nazis in the Sahara?

Shamgar's victory was one of those unnoticed, nearly forgotten battles of the Bible. Your battles and mine are much like his. Every day, we fight in spiritual warfare. Not big, headline-grabbing battles that leave us covered with medals and glory but low-intensity conflicts that usually go unnoticed by the world. We fight our battles against temptation, against our character flaws or laziness, against our sins and bad habits. We fight our low-intensity conflicts against poverty and ignorance. We fight by fostering or adopting a child. We fight by teaching a Sunday school class or helping a teacher in an overcrowded classroom. We fight by volunteering our time, our resources, and extending compassion.

Small battles may not receive medals, awards, or glory, but these victories count in the larger war. God sees, He remembers, and He will reward us for our faithfulness and devotion to duty. While we fight our battles, we mustn't compare ourselves to others. You may not reach the numbers of impoverished people as Mother Teresa did or fight in the social, political, or spiritual battles that Martin Luther King, Jr., E. V. Hill, Billy Graham, or Dietrich Bonhoeffer did. Remember the "Jay, I'm praying for you Charlie?" I haven't seen him in decades, but his prayers and witness live on. My daughters and now my grandchildren live in emotionally healthy households; they love the Lord and bring glory to His name. The cycle of pain has been broken.

Never compare yourself to anyone else. God *"knows the plan I have for you..."* (Jeremiah 29:11) Almighty God personally created you. He does not make mistakes, but He does create individuals. And He intends for every one of us to do great things—great not in the measure of society or culture, but great in that we trust Him to take us beyond our comfort zones and into the unknown by faith.

God has put you strategically on the front lines of His war for human souls. Plant your feet, stay at your post, hold your ground, and fight the battle. He will take care of the war.

Listen for the Call of God

Expectant parents spend weeks searching through baby name books, carefully considering every name, from Aaron and Aaliyah to Zane and Za'Riah (my granddaughter's name.) They want to know how the name sounds and its original meaning.

Similarly, companies pay millions of dollars to PR firms, advertising agencies, and market research

THE POWER OF ONE

professionals to create the right name for their products and corporate identities. The right name can be worth billions. The wrong name can be a marketing disaster, as General Motors discovered when it tried to sell its Chevy Nova automobile in the Latin American market where "no va" in Spanish means "it won't go." The wrong image can destroy a century or more of an excellent reputation, as Anheuser Busch learned when they tried to lean into culture with Tik-Tok transgender star Dylan Mulvaney. The choice was an epic failure with the public.

The names of people in the Bible are frequently used to describe that person's attributes, history, or a promise foretold about the child's future. A person's name often becomes a self-fulfilling prophecy, a preview of life and accomplishments. For example, in Genesis 17, God made a covenant with Abram, saying, *"You will be the father of many nations. No longer will you be called Abram [*which means "Exalted Father"]; *your name will be Abraham* ["Father of Many"]." In 1 Samuel 25, we meet a man named Nabal, described as "surly and mean in his dealings," a man so obnoxious that he insults David, his king. Verse 25 tells us that Nabal "is just like his name—his name is Fool, and folly goes with him." For many characters in the Bible, it's all in a name. The name Shamgar, meaning "stranger" gives us a fascinating glimpse into his background. One thing is evident from the times he lived – Shamgar had to choose the God of Israel even as the thousands around him worshipped myriads of manmade deities. I believe he spent time on the farm earnestly listening for the voice of the One True God and not the culture that clamored around him. He listened for the will of God and obeyed, and that profoundly changed the history of Israel.

To read the Word of God is to begin to hear the voice of God. In our media-drenched age, a surround sound boom of voices shouts for our attention, time, resources, energy, and souls. Practice shutting out these distractions so you can live and walk by Truth. Prayer is a privilege, a two-way conversation. We share our heart and God listens; God speaks, and we hear with an open, willing spirit as He moves and begins to engineer circumstances and relationships.

When you pray, do you find yourself addressing God as if he is your genie in a bottle, talking to him mostly about your needs, wants, and problems? Most often, the voice of God comes first in the Truths already written in the ancient Scriptures. These are your promises to hold on to, memorize, repeat, and live every day, As Deuteronomy 5:22-23 reads, *"So be careful to do what the LORD your God has commanded you; do not turn aside to the right or the left. Walk in obedience to all that the LORD your God has commanded you, so that you may live, prosper, and prolong your days in the land you will possess."*

THE POWER OF ONE

All that you need today, tomorrow, and beyond can be found in the pages of The Book.

When you pray, remember that God is Counselor, Helper, Comforter, and Lord of All. Honor and worship His Majesty and you will find great joy. Psalm 46:10 is one of the "coffee mug" verses we often see: "Be *still and know that I am God.*" In reality, it may be among the most difficult to fulfill. Holding still; thinking deeply; filling our minds with good thoughts is essential to winning any battle in life. Anyone can do it; few make it a habit.

In John 10:27, Jesus says, *"My sheep listen to my voice; I know them, and they follow me."*

In Matthew 6:6, the intimacy of the prayer relationship is unveiled: *"But when you pray, go into your room, close the door, and pray to your Father, who is unseen. Then your Father, who sees what is done in secret, will reward you."*

The Bible is the Book of Life, full of promises, hope, courage, and truth. When you memorize Scripture, you fuel yourself for anything coming your way. James 1:5 says to *"ask for wisdom"* because God loves to give it as a gift. We must stop seeking cheap, easy advice from media or casual friendships. The world is like a carnival, filled with sights, sounds, and bright lights, with dozens of carny barkers shouting at us from their booths, "Try your luck! Don't miss out! Hurry, hurry, hurry, step right this way." False values, destructive philosophies, and deceptive belief systems are offered like free samples. We're tempted to try this and glance at that, enter here and pay our money there—and soon we find that our pockets are turned inside out, our souls are wasted, and we have been played for fools.

The Creator of the Universe, the Lord God Almighty *"has shown you, O mortal, what is good. What does the Lord require of you? To act justly and to love mercy and to walk humbly] with your God."* (Micah 6:8

Keep Cotton in Your Pocket

Author Max Lucado writes, "Ignore what people say. Block them out. Turn them off. Close your ears. And if you have to, walk away. Ignore the ones who say it is too late to start over. Disregard those who say you'll never amount to anything. Turn a deaf ear toward those who say you aren't smart enough, fast enough, tall enough, big enough—ignore them. Faith sometimes begins by stuffing your ears with cotton." History is filled with great people who were told at some time that they would never amount to much.

The well-known failures of President Abraham Lincoln inspire goal setters to get up and try again after a setback. Before becoming president, he failed at two businesses and lost six elections. He failed at his first business in 1831, was defeated for the legislature in 1832, had his second business failure in 1833, suffered a nervous breakdown in 1836, was defeated for speaker in

THE POWER OF ONE

1838, was defeated for elector in 1840, was defeated for Congress in 1843, and again in 1838, was defeated for the Senate in 1855, and was defeated for vice president in 1856—all before finally winning the presidency in 1860.

After his crushing loss in 1855, he said, "The path was worn and slippery. My foot slipped from under me, knocking the other out of the way. But I recovered and said to myself, 'It's a slip and not a fall.'" Well-meaning friends begged him not to run for president, citing another loss would bring more public humiliation. But Lincoln had learned to listen to the voice of God, not the voices of defeat and discouragement. His call to lead the country usurped all else. He was an "ear stuffer" who listened for God's voice and not that of people around him. If he hadn't, America might be two countries today—one nation free and the other comprising slave-owners and their slaves. Lincoln succeeded in ending slavery and holding the nation together.

The infamous Walt Disney stuffed his ears with cotton more than once. His father was a harsh and critical man who continually told young Walter to quit wasting time with his doodling and drawings of farm animals. One of his teachers told him to stop making such ridiculous drawings in class—after all, she said, "Flowers don't have faces!" At age seventeen, Walt served with the Red Cross ambulance corps in France immediately following World War I. When he returned home, his father offered him a job in a Chicago jelly factory. It was a good job and a decent salary for those times, but Walt said, "I don't want to work in a jelly factory. I want to be an artist." "Drawing silly pictures isn't a real job," his father replied.

But seventeen-year-old Walt Disney had a dream, and he wouldn't let his father pour cold water on it. He went to Kansas City and applied to be a cartoonist with the Kansas City Star, where the editor turned him down for being too young. Unfazed, Walt went back the next day and applied for a job as a copyboy, and the advertising manager turned him down for being too old. He then applied at the Kansas City Journal, which also rejected him. Walt finally got a job at a Kansas City commercial art studio, earning $50 monthly. There, she met a young cartoonist, Ub Iwerks, and the two young artists soon founded their own cartoon studio. While Walt and Ub were conducting their first crude experiments with animation, Walt made friends with a little mouse that sometimes ventured out of a hole in the wall. That mouse eventually found its way onto the animation cells that Walt and Ub drew, becoming the beloved Mickey Mouse— 100 years later, the rest is animation history.

When Walt first dreamed of creating the first full-length animated feature, Hollywood experts predicted failure. His grand idea of the world's first theme park was laughed at and deemed a potential financial disaster.

THE POWER OF ONE

Even Walt's wife, Lillian, and brother, Roy, tried to talk him out of his bold dreams. But Walt refused to listen to the critics, the naysayers, the doomsayers, and even his family.

Those who predicted failure were silenced when the movie, Snow White and the Seven Dwarfs, opened with acclaimed popularity. His "Disneyland Theme Park" stunned and excited the world and proved successful beyond even Walt's expectations.

The dramatic tales of how Walt turned his dreams into reality continually astound me. His bios sit on a shelf close to my desk chair because just to see the titles inspires me. When I need a creativity boost, I often make my way to *Magic Kingdom to watch Walt Disney: One Man's Dream.* The 15-minute documentary showcases the life and times of the visionary creator with rare audio recordings and historical footage. Disney is a household name today because Walt refused to listen to his critics.

Albert [26] flunked math in his youth and was labeled a slow learner by his teachers. Fortunately, he stuffed cotton in his ears and became one of the greatest and most influential scientists in history. The brilliant physicist developed the special and general theories of relativity and won the Nobel Prize for Physics in 1921 for his explanation of the photoelectric effect. Einstein is generally considered the most influential physicist of the 20th century. Einstein's brain functioned beyond the normal daily classroom.

And then there was the Great Caruso. As a young man taking private voice lessons, Italian tenor Enrico Caruso was warned that he would never succeed as a singer. "Your voice is like glass," said his teacher. "It cracks on the high notes. It is like gold at the bottom of the Tiber River—not worth digging for. I suggest you save yourself much pain and embarrassment and give up trying to be a singer."

But Caruso would not listen and would not give up. At his debut in Barcelona, his performance was greeted by hissing and booing. After a while, the loudest of his hecklers got up and left, and the remaining audience listened to him in chilly silence. At the end of the performance, there was no applause.

Later, when he sang at the opera house in Salerno, conductor Vincenzo Lombardi came to Caruso's aid. His voice broke when he attempted the high B-flat in the "Flower Song" from Carmen. Lombardi could see the young singer's relentless determination, and he patiently worked with Caruso to build a "top" to his voice. Caruso went on to perform at the Teatro Lirico in Milan, where enthusiastic crowds cheered the fantastic range of his newly extended voice. His triumph spread worldwide, and offers soon poured in from England, America, Russia, across the continent, and throughout Italy—including opera houses where he was previously booed. Enrico Caruso ruled the opera world for decades to come, and after he died, one music critic observed, "The

THE POWER OF ONE

source of Caruso's existence lay only in himself. He was himself the great work of art—the masterpiece."

Theodore Geisel, who became Dr. Seuss, liked to draw but hardly seemed destined for greatness. His high school art teacher told him, "You'll never learn to draw." His Dartmouth College fraternity voted him "Least Likely to Succeed." He went to Oxford to pursue an advanced degree in literature but dropped out due to boredom and restlessness.

Geisel returned to the States and drew cartoons for a struggling magazine (the publication was so cash poor that it paid Geisel in shaving cream and soft drinks instead of money). He also drew comic advertisements for the insecticide product Flit.

Geisel read the report published in LIFE magazine about the problem of illiteracy among American schoolchildren. The reason given was that children's books were boring. Geisel took the challenge. He decided to write a book that would hold children's interest but would only use a basic vocabulary of 220 words. It took him a year and a half to write it, and he published the book under the pen name of Dr. Seuss, now known and loved by millions. That book, The Cat in the Hat, sold 500,000 copies in its first year. The book sold some 16 million copies and counting, even long after his death.

More than 600 million copies of Seuss books have been sold so far. Fortunately for children everywhere,

Geisel refused to be deterred, though his art teacher and college fraternity predicted failure and when forty-three publishers rejected his work. What made him finally able to step out of the crowd and into greatness? He heard of a need in the world – in this case, children learning to read – and he took the challenge to create a viable solution that made him famous. "I can do something about that," he mused. And what were the odds with his background that he could? It didn't matter because what was driving him was a call that matched his purpose and "happy" place, drawing silly pictures and adding silly words.

In your life, there are, or will be, people who could have been your cheerleader and encourager. Instead, they have told you that you will never succeed, so why try? Even if those people are no longer in your life, even if they have been dead for years, you can still hear their voices, criticizing you and making you feel terrible about yourself. Early on, I learned people may be right about my choices, but I have to realize that for myself. You cannot give up because of opinion; you only change course when God leads you.

The Lord has made us uniquely in His image and solely for His glory. He loves you—a Father Who wants the best for His child. If that involves letting you learn the hard way, so be it. We can trust God, always, in every season of life.

The Gift of Sacrifice

There is a moving story in Mark 14 that tells us a lot about the third success secret of Shamgar. Know that your mission will likely require sacrifice of time, money, or social standing. Jesus came to the village of Bethany, near Jerusalem, and stayed in the home of a man named Simon the Leper. While He was at the dinner table, a woman entered the house carrying a jar carved from pure alabaster, a delicate translucent stone, that contained a costly perfume. The woman approached Jesus and did something startling: she deliberately broke the jar. She could have removed the stopper to sprinkle a bit of the fragrance, but she chose to break the jar and pour out the entire contents onto the head of Jesus. The aroma filled the whole house with a bouquet of her love.

Some of those who were present became angry with the woman. They rebuked her aloud and said, "Why did you waste that jar of perfume? It could have been sold for more than a year's wages! The money could have been given to the poor!" Personally, I think they were jealous because her gift could not be matched, and they may have worried that the cost of it would put her in favor with Jesus. *"Leave her alone! Why are you bothering her?"* Jesus replied. *"She has done a beautiful thing for me! You can help the poor anytime you want—but I'm not always going to be here with you."*

Some in the room may not have grasped the meaning of his words. In just a few days, He would be arrested, beaten, demeaned, and nailed to a Roman cross. Her sacrificial gift cost her greatly, but to Jesus, it was a breath of encouragement poured upon Him. Then Jesus said something meant for us to remember: "This woman did what she could." She did what she could!

Her name will never be known, but her legacy lives on. Her story to the crowd was, "Jesus will die, but we will all receive life. I want to be a part of His choice." She couldn't keep Jesus from being betrayed, handed over to the Romans, and crucified. But she did what she could.

How long had she been saving that precious jar of perfume? How long had she kept it hidden so no thief would ever find it? It may have been given to her as a gift when she was born; she saved all those years to use it on her wedding day. We don't know. But we know that when she broke that jar, she sacrificed something incalculably precious.

Jesus went on to declare: "*I tell you the truth, wherever the Gospel is preached throughout the world, what she has done will also be told in memory of her.*" I don't think she ever knew the impact of her story or that it would be written about for generations to come. That is a pure inheritance she has left—no media blitz—just doing "enough."

And there are others after her, many martyrs and selfless givers who have left stories behind to encourage us to stand tall for what and Who we believe in. One of the most memorable for me is Mother Teresa, the Nobel Prize winner Pat spoke of earlier. She gave her tiny frame and huge heart to serve the poorest of the poor and did mighty works in the name of Jesus. At the National Prayer Breakfast in 1994, she turned her face toward President Clinton and said, "Jesus said, 'Anyone who receives a child in my name, receives me.' By adopting a child, these couples receive Jesus but, by aborting a child, a couple refuses to receive Jesus. Please don't kill the child. I want the child. Please give me the child. I am willing to accept any child who would be aborted and to give that child to a married couple who will love the child and be loved by the child."

Knowing that the President of the United States condoned abortion, she bravely, but humbly, confronted him. Her genuine love and boldness always presented together. Character lives on to multiply into the next generation. I hope you are in that group.

My dear friends, Bill and Vonette Bright, embodied the definitions of faithfulness and focus for me and countless others. While studying at Princeton and Fuller Theological Seminaries, Bright says he was inspired to leave his budding business empire and embrace the scriptural command to "go and make disciples of all the nations" (Matthew 28:19).

Bill Bright and his wife Vonette pursued their passion for ministry by starting CRU at the University of

California in Los Angeles. What began with college students has since grown over half a century to become the world's most extensive international Christian ministry, reaching beyond students to serve inner cities, the military, athletes, political and business leaders, the entertainment industry, and families. After being awarded the Templeton Prize worth more than $1 million for progress in religion, Dr Bright quickly donated all prize money to causes promoting the spiritual benefits of fasting and prayer.

My greatest moment with Bill Bright was sitting in his living room talking about dreams and disappointments. "Jay, do you know how many years I prayed for someone to help me with the Jesus film?" I shook my head slightly and leaned in. "Forty years of asking for help to bring the vision to life, and 40 years of being told 'no.' Forty years of praying for the vision and call of God to come true." That true story deeply influences me in decision-making and reaching for goals. The Jesus Film has been seen by more than 11 billion people and more than 665 million around the globe indicated a decision for Christ after watching it.[27] It was definitely worth the four-decade wait.

There are no "instant coffee" great dreams. They are thought through in length, prayed over in earnest, strengthened with grit and hard work, and waited, waited, waited upon. As Bill told me, it is what happens in the waiting that is more significant and life-defining than when the goal comes to fruition. I have found that to be true.

These have left behind a legacy that many will not recognize by name as the years go by, but countless will live on to multiply their stories of faithfulness. We could travel throughout history to "see" what faithfulness married with humility looks like – Peter and Stephen martyred; Mary and Joseph risking their lives; Dr. Martin Luther King; Alexander Solzhenitsyn; William Wilberforce, and thousands of unnamed missionaries serving across the planet. You may be thinking of several as you read this. Their names are sometimes not remembered or often mentioned, but their legacy lives and breathes on.

Four centuries after Jesus walked the Earth, a quiet monk from Asia named Telemachus believed God called him to walk from what was probably the country of Turkey to Rome, Italy, more than 2,000 land miles and across two bodies of water, to try and put an end to the inhumane persecution and murder of Christians. On the day he arrived, some 50,000 spectators were crowded into the Colosseum amphitheater to watch the spectacles of blood and cruelty by gladiators, cheering them on with frenzied shouts of approval. The gladiators fought against enraged wild animals and murdered helpless humans, all for sport as a sort of military victory parade under the rule of the 20-year-old Emperor Honorius. The Voice of the Martyrs tells of his outcry: "Telemachus jumped from the crowd into the arena itself, no longer spectator but activist, peacemaker, preacher. 'Do not requite God's mercy,' he screamed, 'in turning away the swords of your enemies by murdering each other!'"

As one would expect, no one paid attention. Next, Telemachus positioned himself between the gladiators as he begged them to stop. The crowd roared, "This is no place for preaching! The old customs of Rome must be observed! On, gladiators!" This in no way deterred Telemachus as he continued his pursuit of stopping the slaughters and bloody battles. Within minutes, an impatient gladiator thrust a sword into Telemachus' body. As he fell dead onto the arena floor, the spectators threw stones.[28]

The spectacle made news throughout Rome, even to Emperor Honorius, that the gentle monk was coldly murdered. Was his courage a loss? No, it was not. His story of boldness to speak of mercy in the name of God changed the culture. Honorius stopped the savage games. The quiet monk has been described as one "whose death was more useful to mankind than his life."[29]

Telemachus had no team to count on and no financial backing for his call, but he did what he could. As Jesus said of the woman, "It was enough." You do not have to be a martyr to leave a legacy, but you do have to be willing to show valiant guts in front of the opposition and stand for the truth of the Faithful God. As with many of those we discussed, Shamgar included, they never knew how great their legacy would be.

We don't need a guarantee that what we do daily will land in history books or social media. Testimonies of faith multiply through people. We do need to be sure we have done with all our might that which has been instilled in us. The rest we leave for generations to come.

No Excuses

While my friend Bob Wieland was studying at the University of Wisconsin, he was negotiating for a job as a pitcher with the Philadelphia Phillies. But Bob's pro baseball career was interrupted before it started when he received a letter of greetings from Uncle Sam. The U.S. government had decided he was needed in Vietnam.

While serving in the Vietnam War, he became involved in a fierce firefight. One of his buddies was wounded, and Bob ran to his aid—but he didn't see the 82 mm mortar round that was right in his path. He stepped on it, and the round exploded, tearing off both of his legs. Bob was taken to a field hospital where the doctors pronounced him DOA—dead on arrival. But a few minutes later, someone noticed that Bob still had a slight pulse.

Bob Weiland arrived in Vietnam weighing 200 pounds and standing six feet tall. He returned home weighing only 87 pounds, his body almost cut in half as a double amputee. Some people thought that Bob's life was over. Bob disagreed by saying, "My legs went one direction, my life another."

The moment the doctors released him from intensive care, Bob started to focus on his rehabilitation. To compensate for the loss of his legs, he began strength training on his arms and upper body. He wasn't going to be immobilized by a mortar round. Bob Wieland chose to focus on the future. He would go wherever he wanted, even if he had to get there by walking on his hands. Eight years later, weighing just 122 pounds, Wieland competed in the United States Power Lifting Championship. He broke the world record by lifting 303 pounds—then was told by the judges that he was disqualified. Someone checked the rule book and found that all contestants must wear shoes. Bob's quick reply: "Wouldn't you know? Today would be the day I forgot my shoes!"

Bob has completed some of the most amazing treks in history using a customized pair of pads to cushion his fists. He began his "Spirit of America" walk at Independence Hall in Knotts Berry Farm and completed his journey at the Vietnam Memorial in Washington, D.C. The entire walk, accomplished entirely on his hands, took three years, eight months, six days, and nearly five million "hand steps."[30]

He walked over concrete freeways, steel bridges, asphalt streets, and gravel roads—and he did it all by simply putting one hand in front of the other. Bob

THE POWER OF ONE

continued his trek regardless of ice storms or desert heat. Sometimes, his way was lined with cheering spectators, but there were also times when people heckled him. On one occasion, a carful of rowdy teens drove by, pelting him with water balloons. When a reporter asked him what motivated him for such a long and arduous hike, he replied, "The Bible says, 'Delight yourself in the Lord and he will give you the desires of your heart.' That's what keeps me going."

Weiland became the only double amputee to compete in the demanding Ironman Triathlon in Kona, Hawaii. He completed the grueling multisport competition by using his arms to propel him one step at a time toward the finish line. Bob completed the Los Angeles Marathon in 173 hours and 45 minutes and "ran" the New York and Marine Corps Marathon. He has broken the world record for the bench press four times, stunning the world by pressing 507 pounds. Weiland has twice completed a 6,200-mile bike circuit across America. He was recognized as "The Most Courageous Man in America" by the NFL Players Association and the Jim Thorpe Foundation, has served as a consultant to the President's Council on Physical Fitness and Sports, and much more. President Reagan dubbed him "Mr. Inspiration." More impressive than Bob's feats of physical endurance is his incredible faith. He credits his achievements to the Lord, who gives him the strength to take each step and live joyfully and gratefully. Bob could have sunk into bitterness and despair. Still, he made a deliberate choice to start where he was (a VA hospital) and use what he had (two good arms) to do what he could (months of intensive therapy and training, followed by one incredible feat after another). Bob didn't just want to settle—he wanted to soar!

I first met Bob Weiland when I tripped over him on the sidelines of a preseason NFL game. I felt terrible, falling all over myself with apologies. Bob smiled and stuck out a hand of friendship. He was introduced to me as the strength coach for the Green Bay Packers, and I knew immediately this was no ordinary guy.

Bob and I often spoke at the same conference and became good friends and close brothers. I remember the morning we planned to work out together before our next event. I had a bum knee, having had surgery but needing a repeat. The morning after speaking at 5 or 6 schools and a crusade, I called Bob to say, "Man, I can't make it. My knee is killing me." I will never forget what he said, "You have a knee? What does that feel like? I wish I had a knee and could feel it hurt." That hit me hard, and I walked out the door to work out with Bob. We all need that kind of friend, one who accepts no excuses.

What about you? What do you want to do with the rest of your life? And what's stopping you? What obstacles are in your way? What barriers do you have to cross to reach your goal? Bob Wieland is living proof that most obstacles and barriers are only in our minds.

THE POWER OF ONE

As Bob said, "I lost my legs, not my heart." If a man without legs can do what he's done, then you and I have no excuses.

Life is a marathon. You may not think you can finish, but I know you can. You can overcome any opposition, any obstacle, even six-hundred-to-one odds, to reach your goal.

EPILOGUE

It's Your Move.

"Life is a game board. Time is your opponent. If you procrastinate you will lose the game. You must make a move to be victorious." Napoleon Hill

God has a plan for this entire universe, and you are a part of that plan. He knew you by name before He created the world and saved a spot with your name when He fit together all the millions of pieces of His design. As Zach Williams sings in his song "Rescue Story," "You were writing the pages before I had a name; before I needed grace…" God has called you to do a task. I don't know what that task is, but I do know this: If you don't do it, it may never be done. And, who knows how your willingness to wait and risk and care may have changed the course of history if you had only said, "Yes, Lord."

In John 17:20-21, Jesus gave His plan for continuing the message of Good News once He was gone from the earth: *"I am praying not only for these disciples but also for all who will ever believe in me through their message. I pray that they will all be one, just as you and I are one—as you are in me, Father, and I am in you. And may they be in us so that the world will believe you sent me."*

When you consider this passage, the privilege is a heavy one. Jesus willingly gave His life on the cross, conquered death, physically rose from the dead, returned to glory, and left us to continue His work.

An ancient fable corresponds to these verses: "On the day of Pentecost, Jesus was taken up into heaven. Upon his arrival, the angels gathered around and asked him how his work would continue on the earth without him. "Oh," Jesus said, "I have a plan. I have left my disciples on the earth. They will share the Gospel with other people. Those people will hear the story of my love for them, and they will become my disciples, too. And they will tell other people, who will tell other people, who will tell other people. Faith will spread around the world, and many will come to believe in me. That is my plan." The angels blinked in surprise. "You mean," they said, "you are trusting human beings to carry out your plan? You know how unreliable they are! You know how easily they become discouraged and fall into laziness!" "Yes," Jesus said, "I know all that." "But what if they let you down? What will you do then?" "I don't know," Jesus said. "I have no other plan."

It's true. Jesus has entrusted the future of the human race to us – to pray, to serve, to tell the story of His love. He created you with gifts, talents, strengths, and weaknesses. You are unique. Throughout life, you will find yourself using those gifts in front of people others may never meet. You and I each have our role to fulfill.

THE POWER OF ONE

If the young man in my senior high school class had not said, "Jay, I am praying for you to know Jesus," my life would have been drastically different, and not in a good way. God's plan hinges on your obedience and willingness to care for your neighbor as you do for yourself. There is no other plan.

Sometimes I believe the greatest creativity of mankind comes in the imagination of excuses. There are always reasons why "it won't work; it can't be done, I'll think about it later," etc. And perhaps the greatest excuse of all - "There is no way out, no more moves. I have tried everything."

I haven't played much these days, but I remember a tense chess game at Skibo Castle in Scotland against my friend, Matt Crouch, President of Trinity Broadcast Network (TBN). As a novice chess player, I refused to submit a loss to Matt (only because it would be brought up years later, as it has) and could feel the heavy frustration of being trapped. Decades later, there is still a debate over who won.

A chess player may spend hour upon hour looking for that "one more move," and that in itself may be the attraction of the game. I came across the story of the famous "Checkmate" painting by Friedrich August Moritz Retzsch some years ago. The original story, "Anecdote of Morphy," referred to the erudite chess player Paul Morphy of the late 1800's. The writer tells it much better than I could, so I will quote directly from Columbia Chess Chronicle, dated August 18, 1888.[31]

"...An invitation was extended to the champion (Morphy), and with himself at the centre, a coterie of notables assembled for an evening's play at the home of the hospitable Mr. H...While at supper Morphy's attention was attracted by a picture which hung prominently upon the wall...It represents the politely despised Mephistopheles (the Devil) playing a game of chess with a young man for his soul. The Chessmen with which his Satanic Majesty plays are the Vices; the pieces of the young man are, or have been, the Virtues - for alas he has very few left.... The unhappy youth...appears not only desperate but hopeless, and his fate is sealed. His adversary gloats in anticipation of the final coup, and the gleaming smile on the face of the latter intensifies the despair which that of the young man shows.

With the close of supper, deeply interested, Morphy approached the picture, studied it awhile intently, then turning to his host he said modestly: 'I think that I can take the young man's game and win.... Suppose we place the men and try...' To the surprise of everyone, victory was snatched from the devil and the young man saved."

In life, the pieces placed before us show many possible moves, but the difference is that we need not be a master to win against evil. We have already been given more than we need:

THE POWER OF ONE

"A final word: Be strong in the Lord and in his mighty power. Put on all of God's armor so that you will be able to stand firm against all strategies of the devil. For we are not fighting against flesh-and-blood enemies, but against evil rulers and authorities of the unseen world, against mighty powers in this dark world, and against evil spirits in the heavenly places. Therefore, put on every piece of God's armor so you will be able to resist the enemy in the time of evil. Then after the battle you will still be standing firm." Eph 6:10-13

The next verse has traveled with me across the country and around the globe. With every snare of the devil placed before me, I recite it and run from whatever or whoever.

"The temptations in your life are no different from what others experience. And God is faithful. He will not allow the temptation to be more than you can stand. When you are tempted, he will show you a way out so that you can endure." 1 Corinthians 10:13

According to CNBC, our states are holding $70 billion in unclaimed assets.[32] The wisdom and promises given in the Scripture are luxurious estates loaded with more than you will ever come close to exhausting. Faith loses to hopelessness when we do not access the gifts we have already been given and defeat soon follows. We stop believing in options. Let it not be so!

Christ gave His life to become your Personal Savior, one who will never give up on you, stop loving you, or cease chasing after you. He rushes in with strength and endurance when you even think of giving in. He will never fail, but you and I might if we give up or give in because we leave the abundance of wisdom and strength unclaimed. No matter what opponents or obstacles you face right now, there is always one crucial move you can still make.

Start where you are, use what you have, and do what you can. *My friend, it's your move.*

About the Authors

PAT WILLIAMS was the former Executive Senior Vice President of the Orlando Magic of the NBA, a basketball team he co-founded in 1987. Pat was involved in professional sports for forty-three years. He was one of America's top motivational and inspirational speakers and the author of more than forty books. He and his wife, Ruth, have nineteen children, including fourteen adopted from four foreign countries.

JAY STRACK is the founder of Student Leadership University and the Center for Global Leadership at Charleston Southern University. Jay has addressed students, educators, corporate groups, government agencies, and professional sports teams with the message, "If I can overcome, anyone can." Dr. Strack served on the President's Anti-Drug Task Force under Presidents Ronald Reagan and George H. W. Bush and as a faith advisor to the White House during the Trump administration. Contact: @Jstrack007

Endnotes:

[1] *Shamgar - Hitchcock's Bible Names Dictionary online.* (n.d.). Bible Study Tools. https://www.biblestudytools.com/dictionaries/hitchcocks-bible-names/shamgar.html

[2] *Anath: Bible.* (n.d.). Jewish Women's Archive. https://jwa.org/encyclopedia/article/anath-bible#:~:text=Anath%20(Anat)%20is%20a%20prominent,fertility%20and%20storm%20god%20Baal.

[3] Forward. (2017, September 25). *The real history of the name "Palestine"* The Forward. https://forward.com/opinion/letters/383433/the-real-history-of-the-name-palestine/

[4] The Editors of Encyclopaedia Britannica. (2024, February 29). *Philistine | Definition, People, Homeland, & Facts.* Encyclopedia Britannica. https://www.britannica.com/topic/Philistine-people

[5] Gender identity. (2022, February 8). Teen Talk. https://teentalk.ca/learn-about/gender-identity/#:~:text=There%20are%20many%20different%20gender,identities%20then%20we%27ve%20listed.

6 The Editors of Encyclopedia Britannica. (1998, July 20). *Moloch | Definition & Facts*. Encyclopedia Britannica. https://www.britannica.com/topic/Moloch-ancient-god

7 *BBC NEWS | Entertainment | Rodin sculpture stolen*. (n.d.). http://news.bbc.co.uk/2/hi/entertainment/2949436.stm

8 *Introduction to 2 Timothy | ESV.org*. (n.d.). ESV Bible. https://www.esv.org/resources/esv-global-study-bible/introduction-to-2-timothy/

9 *Lysippos (The J. Paul Getty Museum Collection). (n.d.). https://www.getty.edu/art/collection/perMonument to the Burghers of Calais,son/103JQM*

10. *Statuette of Alexander the Great (The J. Paul Getty Museum Collection). (n.d.). https://www.getty.edu/art/collection/object/103SXQ*

THE POWER OF ONE

---

[11] *Horatio Nelson | Royal Navy*. (n.d.). https://www.royalnavy.mod.uk/news-and-latest-activity/features/trafalgar-day/horatio-nelson#:~:text=Horatio%20Nelson%20is%20generally%20regarded,%27Britannia%27s%20God%20of%20War%27.

[12] https://www.gutenberg.ca/ebooks/lewiscs-screwtapeletters/lewiscs-screwtapeletters-00-h.html

[13] *G3670 - homologeō - Strong's Greek Lexicon (kjv)*. (n.d.). Blue Letter Bible. https://www.blueletterbible.org/lexicon/g3670/kjv/tr/0-1/

[14] *Alexander Solzhenitsyn*. (n.d.). Spartacus Educational. https://spartacus-educational.com/RUSsolzhenitsyn.htm

[15] *Life Story | Arthur Ashe Legacy*. (n.d.). Arthur Ashe Legacy. https://arthurashe.ucla.edu/life-story/

[16] *Ronald Reagan and the collapse of the Soviet Empire*. (n.d.). https://ciaotest.cc.columbia.edu/olj/ad/ad_v9_3/sef01.html

[17] NASA. (2023, July 26). Apollo 13: Mission Details - NASA. *NASA.* https://www.nasa.gov/mission/apollo-13/

[18] Pastor reflects on his "Mama's" love and prayers. (n.d.). Preaching Today. https://www.preachingtoday.com/illustrations/2011/may/2050211.html#:~:text=As%20he%20was%20growing%20up,that%20he%20go%20to%20college.

[19] The Editors of Encyclopaedia Britannica. (2024a, February 17). *Jethro Tull | Agricultural Revolution, seed drill & Inventor.* Encyclopedia Britannica. https://www.britannica.com/biography/Jethro-Tull

[20] *Mother Teresa of Calcutta – Mother Teresa of Calcutta Catholic School. (n.d.). https://mtctampa.org/mother-teresa-of-calcutta/#:~:text=Although%20she%20struggled%20to%20find,the%20poorest%20children%20in%20Calcutta*

[21] *nMarsden, G.nM. (2016). C. S. Lewis's "Mere Christianity." In Princeton University Press eBooks. https://doi.org/10.1515/9781400880492*

[22] Kim, K. (2022, May 30). Inspirational Leadership quotes | Voltaire. *Laidlaw Scholars Network*. https://laidlawscholars.network/posts/everyone-is-guilty-of-all-the-good-they-did-not-do

[23] Hauser, T. (2024, March 11). *Muhammad Ali | Biography, Bouts, Record, & Facts*. Encyclopedia Britannica. https://www.britannica.com/biography/Muhammad-Ali-boxer

[24] Marshall, C. (2024, January 15). *How Martin Luther King Jr. got C's in Public Speaking–Before becoming a Straight-A student and a world class orator*. Open Culture.
   https://www.openculture.com/2020/12/how-martin-luther-king-jr-went-from-getting-cs-on-his-report-card-even-in-public-speaking-to-straight-as.html#google_vignette

[25] Walter, G. (2018, November 19). Why can't I use general purpose duct tape on HVAC ductwork? *Tape University®*.
https://tapeuniversity.com/industry/hvac-industry/why-cant-i-use general-purpose-duct-tape-on-ductwork/

[26] Kaku, M. (2024, March 10). *Albert Einstein | Biography, Education, Discoveries, & Facts*. Encyclopedia Britannica. https://www.britannica.com/biography/Albert-Einstein

[27] *Jesus Film Project Statistics [Updated] July 2022*. (n.d.). Jesus Film Project. https://www.jesusfilm.org/partners/resources/strategies/statistics/

[28] Megan. (2021, October 25). *Stories of Christian Martyrs: Telemachus –stories*. Stories. https://www.persecution.com/stories/stories-of-christian-martyrs-telemachus/

[29] *Work info: History of the Decline and Fall of the Roman Empire - Christian Classics Ethereal Library*. (n.d.). https://www.ccel.org/ccel/g/gibbon/decline/

[30] Wikipedia contributors. (2023, November 25). *Bob Wieland* Wikipedia. https://en.wikipedia.org/wiki/Bob_Wieland

[31] *One more Move--Paul Morphy Beats the Devil at Chess.* (n.d.). https://www.one-more-move-chess-art.com/One-MoreMove.html

[32] O'Brien, S. (2023, February 1). States have $70 billion in unclaimed assets. How to check if any is yours. *CNBC.* https://www.cnbc.com/2023/02/01/how-to-check-if-youre-owed-a-share-of-70-billion-in-unclaimed-assets.html

Find more information on virtual, domestic, or international premier Student Leadership programs that teach how to Think, Dream, and Lead at https://slulead.com

For information on online courses through Strack Center for Global Leadership at the distinctive Charleston Southern University, go to https://www.charlestonsouthern.edu/academics/strack-center/

www.ingramcontent.com/pod-product-compliance
Lightning Source LLC
Chambersburg PA
CBHW060738050426
42449CB00008B/1265